THE

and

INTELLIGENT

she

WOMAN'S

lived

GUIDE TO

happily

ONLINE

ever after

DATING

BY DALE KOPPEL, PhD.

Published by: Peterman, Samuelson Publishing, LLC
Rockport, MA. 01966

For more information,
visit www.theintelligentwomansguide.com

ISBN-978-0-615-24247-7

Printed in the United States of America

About

PETERMAN, SAMUELSON PUBLISHING, LLC

Many people ask me why I self-published *The Intelligent Woman's Guide To Online Dating*. After all, there's such a stigma these days about self-publishing. People automatically assume that a self-published book is one that's been submitted to, and rejected by, "real" publishers. That's not true with this book. I never approached publishers. I wanted to publish it myself. Like my philosophy about online dating, I had the same philosophy on publishing this book: Why wait? The book was done; I liked it. I thought it read well and would be enjoyed, exactly as it was, by others. And I loved the "flip over" – two books in one – idea. I was afraid that a "real" publisher would want to take a more traditional approach, and I'd be devastated. After all, I'm not traditional; how I approached online dating and ended up with Mr. Right wasn't traditional; my advice isn't traditional. So why should my book have a traditional format?

The hardest part was coming up with a name for my publishing "house." I rejected the obvious: My initials; my last name; my first pet's name. I wanted the name to sound "professional," maybe even a little British. Peterman, Samuelson Publishing, LLC. After all, Peter is my man, and Samuel is his son. Now you know.

CONTENTS

How To Read This Book   ix

Preface   xiii

Acknowledgments   xvii

CHAPTER ONE:

    INTRODUCTION: HOW I DID IT   1

CHAPTER TWO:

    FIRST, THE PHOTOS: HOW I DID IT   7

CHAPTER THREE:

    NEXT, THE PROFILE: HOW I DID IT   11

CHAPTER FOUR:

    TROLLING FOR MEN: HOW I DID IT

    Step 1: The Search   27

    Step 2: The Initial Contact   40

    Step 3: Hopefully, The Response   41

    Step 4: The Meeting   43

CHAPTER FIVE:

    WHAT ABOUT SEX: HOW I DID IT   61

CHAPTER SIX:

    OH, THE MEN I MET   69

CHAPTER SEVEN:

    AND SHE LIVED HAPPILY EVER AFTER   93

HOW TO READ THIS BOOK

This is a "flip-over" book. Two books in one. One side – the side you're on now – tells my story. How I found my "Mr. Right," right online. Flip it over to the other side, and you'll find the book that tells how you can do it, too.

You can read this book in two ways:

You can read this entire side first (how I did it), then go to the flip side of the book (how you can do it, too), and read it in its entirety. Or you can go from one chapter on this side to the corresponding chapter on the other side. Back and forth; back and forth. You decide.

No matter how you navigate it, read both sides of the book as you would any other "How-To" book. Critically. What resonates for you? What doesn't? You want to get from Point A to Point B, but you need to create your own way of doing it, your own road map.

I wrote this side of the book to show you that it can be done. How inspirational is that?

For me, it was all about giving myself permission to do it in a way that worked for me. And only me. I did it with gusto and determination and a truly positive and confident attitude, even during the times I really wasn't feeling positive and confident. Being positive didn't mean that I wasn't disappointed – sometimes again and again; it meant that I wouldn't give up until I'd accomplished my goal(s), which was not always the goal(s) I had started out with.

I realized that by doing it right (for me), I could always feel in control, which was important to me. It was a mindset that I cultivated and worked at. And it worked.

I wrote the other side of this book to show you that you can do it, too. How motivational is that? Now, it's up to you to pick apart the way I did it. You can decide to do it in a totally different way–and still succeed.

It's all about giving yourself permission to do it in a way that works for you. And only you. Just make sure that you do it with gusto and determination and a truly positive and confident attitude, even when you're not necessarily feeling positive or confident. Being positive doesn't mean that you won't be disappointed–sometimes again and again; it means that you won't give up until you've accomplished your goal(s), which may not be the goal(s) you started out with. If you do it right (for you), you will always feel in control. It's a mindset that you may have never had before, but it's possible to develop and cultivate it now. And you will.

I am thrilled to be able to share my story–a three-year saga–with you.

But first read the preface, written by one of the 100-plus men I met online.

PREFACE

By Steve Edelheit

Dale was attractive, funny, smart, easily the most engaging woman I'd met online. She was also, as it turned out, quite frank and to the point. I was more than a little disappointed when she told me she wasn't interested.

It was our third date after meeting through Match.com. Now, third dates can be turning points, and I admit I had been looking forward to it. So, it came as something of a surprise when Dale looked at me across the table and said, "You know we're not going to have a romantic relationship, don't you?" I didn't know that; in fact, I was kind of hoping it would turn into something lively, sexy, and consuming.

But then she cocked her head, smiled, and said, "We could be great friends, though." Much to my surprise, this surprising woman meant just that. And our friendship has been one of the best things to come out of my online experience.

What led me to respond to Dale's profile out of the some 600 that popped up in my search? Well, for one thing, it wasn't the standard "nice, honest, kind person looking for a nice, honest, kind guy" kind of presentation. It was unusual; it was funny; it was a quiz. I read the first couple of questions:

1) You see the glass (a) half full (b) half empty (c) You can't see the glass.

2) You think (a) out of the box (b) inside the box (c) What box?

And I was hooked. Of course, like most men, I had already taken a careful look at her photos. There were a lot of them, showing both profile and full body shots, some of Dale in full dress-up mode and others of her in work-out clothes and yoga poses. (You see what an impression they made on me? I can still remember them.) The message was: I may not be perfect, but I'm more than OK. I've gone to some trouble to have really good pictures taken, and I like myself enough to show you the self I am and like. And I'm confident enough to believe you'll like me, too. The combination of photos and profile was enough for me to know I had to meet this woman.

As a friend these last few years, Dale has entertained and amazed me with her tales of life online. But it wasn't just the amusing stories of dates gone bad, it was that in addition to being funny, she could be so perceptive and knowing about what went wrong and about how to make it right, and about how to get the most out of her time online – or, for that matter, anyone's time online.

After listening to my own tales of disappointment, puzzlement, and strangeness, Dale would always offer the punchy, irreverent, but always wise, advice that I quickly came to rely on. It's this advice that you'll find in this book. The practical advice that she imparts with the positive, coaxing, saucy attitude that sounds so much like the Dale I know – the experienced, tough, but heart-in-the-right-place friend we all want to have when we have doubts about ourselves and don't know whether or how to do something.

And now you, too, can have the benefit of this funny, wise friend and guide to help you get out there and make the most of your online dating experience. So, what are you waiting for?

ACKNOWLEDGMENTS

This book is dedicated to:

My plastic surgeon, for making me look – and feel – younger.

My cosmetic dentist, for giving me a smile that I could be proud of.

My Pilates instructor, for giving me a great Pilates body.

My yoga teachers, for giving me flexibility of mind, so that I could stay calm and focused on my goal(s) – even during the worst of times, and flexibility of body, so that I could be great in bed.

My friends, for asking questions but never questioning my motives (well, almost never), and for listening to my tales.

My mother/my role model/my confidante, for her unconditional love, support, and inspiration.

My mother's boyfriend, for showing me that there are still great men out there.

My ex-husband, for loving me and leaving me. If it weren't for him, this book wouldn't exist.

The hundred-plus men I met online – especially Peter, for giving this book its happy ending.

BOOK ONE:
HOW I DID IT

CHAPTER ONE

Introduction:
How I Did It

April 4, 2004. Boca Raton, Florida. My husband and I split up after almost 25 years of a wonderful marriage. I never expected it to end. He was leaving me for a man.

Twelve days later, after considering my options (sit at home alone, watching *Sex and the City* reruns; hang out at bars; mope), I joined jdate.com. It was the online dating site that, after looking through others, I thought was the one most suited to who I was and what I was looking for.

"Don't you think you should go through a mourning period first?" my well-meaning friends asked me.

"What do I have to mourn about?" I replied. "I've had a wonderful marriage. He's not coming back. What am I waiting for? Life's too short."

Within seconds of posting my photos and profile, I had guys checking me out. One guy was already instant messaging me. On-line dating veterans refer to these men as "hawks," swooping down on women who are brand new to the site – the "newbies" who have just come onboard.

"Hi *DJK123* (the online name I had chosen). What's cookin?" he wrote. I was blown away by the instantaneous attention.

We messaged back and forth for about 20 minutes, he getting to know me better; I, him. Wow, isn't this fun!

And then, he wrote, "Got any grandkids?"

I wrote back, "No."

Then . . .

Nothing. He was gone.

Wait a minute! What was going on here?

"If you're so into someone having grandkids, why didn't you ask me that question right off the bat instead of wasting my time?" I speed-typed. But it was too late. He was really gone.

And that was my initiation into the wacky world of online dating. From there, it was a veritable roller coaster ride. The highs, the lows, the lowers. One step forward, two steps back. Or so it often seemed. But I persevered, and I took notes. Maybe this will turn into a book someday, I thought. In the meantime, "journaling" was therapeutic. It reminded me of how I had felt as a teenager writing in my white leatherette diary, the one with the tiny lock and key.

Wednesday: Dear Diary, I just met the cutest boy. He asked me out for Saturday. I think I'm in love.

Saturday: Dear Diary, He stood me up. Boys suck. If you never hear from me again, it's because I'm going to slit my wrists.

Those were the days when my mother would tell me, "Don't worry. There are many fish in the sea," even though in those days, it simply wasn't true. If you broke up with a boyfriend, it could take years before you met someone else. Hence, the tendency to stick with it. So, he didn't like your best friend. Were you going to leave him over that? No, not when you considered the alternative. Maybe he had some bad habits. Were you going to end the relationship over those? No, not when you considered the alternative.

The alternative is different now, thanks to online dating. My mother is finally right. There really are hundreds of fish in the sea. The online sea. No, make that tens of thousands. In a three-year period, over 3,000 men had looked at my profile. I probably looked at twice as many men's profiles. I actually met over 100 of them, face-to-face. What an abundance of opportunities. What a sense of power. I was totally in control. I could make my own choices. I loved it!

There were times when I could – and would – meet three new men in a day – one for breakfast or morning coffee; one for lunch or afternoon coffee; one for drinks or dinner. Or drinks first, then dinner if the drinks went well.

I felt like a kid in a candy store, my eyes popping out of my head as I scanned the massive glass showcases and thought to myself, "What an incredible assortment! Look at all different sizes, shapes, and flavors."

My life really had become a box of chocolates!

In my online dating candy store, the potential for a better piece of candy was only a computer click away. How easy. How seductive. How destructive. One false move and it was back to the box of chocolates.

Eeny, Meeny, Miney, Moe. And Curly and Larry, too. And Gary and Barry and Harry, and oh so many others. I had them all.

*N*ow, continue to the next chapter, or flip this book over to page 1 to see how you can do it, too.

CHAPTER TWO

First, The Photos:
How I Did It

Iwas an ugly teen-ager and therefore, as one might expect, very unpopular with the boys. It was the worst of times. Photos taken during that time period typically showed me scowling. But, according to my mother, I had a nice personality. Looking back, I'm not even sure of that.

Though my looks had improved over the years, thanks to cosmetic dentistry and plastic surgery, I still found myself intimidated by the lens of the camera and the idea that men were going to be judging me online by how I looked. Not by my "nice" personality.

I had my daughter take the photos for jdate.com, and I felt really awkward. I became quickly frustrated and ended the photo session. "They're good enough," I told her. Clearly, that was the wrong attitude.

About nine months later, I cancelled my jdate.com membership, took a short breather, then joined Match.com. This time, I took the photo process seriously. Very seriously. I asked a friend of mine – a man I had met on jdate – if he would take the photos. He was not only amenable but also very supportive and patient and fun. He was honest, too, which was essential. We had a great time, and the photos reflected it. I looked relaxed and happy.

I treated it as a photo shoot–different backgrounds, varied attire. (See the back cover of this book for some examples.) I chose to wear tight-fitting jeans with very sexy, very high heels, because I wanted to show that I, in fact, had a seductive side. I posed in a sexy black dress that exposed my shoulders. I put on leggings and a halter top and got into a yoga pose to demonstrate my flexibility, and, yes, to show (off) my body. I knew I was taking a risk by putting myself out there this way, but I decided it was worth it. If I got a bad response, the solution was easy. Take some or, if necessary, all of the full-body photos down and replace them with more conventional photos. But I never felt the need to take them down. From the beginning, men's comments were positive and appropriate, though I could immediately identify the jaded ones–those who had been burned too many times by women who didn't look at all like their photos. Those were the men who would say, "Great photos," and then . . . "Is that really how you look 'now'?" The operative word being 'now,' of course. Being able to honestly respond in the affirmative was critical.

*N*ow, continue to the next chapter, or flip this book over to page 9 to see how you can do it, too.

CHAPTER THREE

Next, The Profile:
How I Did It

Jdate.com may have been my initial online dating site of choice, but I didn't especially like its profile format. It was more about filling-in-the-blanks and choosing multiple-choice answers than about writing an essay that gave me a chance to express myself. Even the freestyle sections limited the amount I could say about myself. Now, for people who don't like to write, this must have been a relief. It felt inhibiting to me. Or maybe it was just my attitude. The truth was, as badly as I wanted to get this thing started, I was intimidated and scared, and pissed off – and sad – that I found myself suddenly single.

But I tackled the profile – category by category.

For "About Me," I wrote:

Freelance writer/real estate developer who wants to do it all, sometimes all at once. I love to travel, eat out, go to the movies, theater, and concerts.

(Hey, I thought, it's short and to-the-point. As I look back at it, I wonder whether the *wants to do it all, sometimes all at once* might have been too intimidating to the men who read it.)

For "Perfect Match," I wrote:

I'm looking for a man who is involved in a career that he loves, is intelligent, optimistic, fit, with a sense of humor, and a zest for life. Someone who doesn't take life too seriously, except when absolutely necessary.

(I liked the way that sounded, although I probably would have rather–I wouldn't have been the only one–written something about how stupid the question was. But then I didn't want to come across as negative because that's not who I am.)

For "Ideal Relationship," I wrote:

The ideal relationship is one in which two people are able to communicate openly, treat each other with respect, share common interests, but allow the other person to be a unique individual.

(Here, I thought, is another stupid question. Is there really an "Ideal Relationship"? Or, for that matter, a "Perfect Match"? Or the "Perfect First Date," which was the next category.)

Initially, I wrote:

A perfect first date is one that's casual and comfortable, one that's in a setting that's conducive to talking.

Later, after having a few first–and second–dates, I added:

However, I think the real first date is the second date.

(In other words, I felt as though first dates were all about good behavior. True colors started coming out on the second dates.)

For "Learned from Past Experiences," I wrote:

You can never be too kind or too respectful of the other person. If you're with the right person, it's a piece of cake. If you feel like you have to work too hard at it, then it's not the right relationship.

(Blah, blah, blah. The reality is, I thought to myself, he will never even read this. Or care what I wrote. For men, it's all about the photos; if he likes my photos, he'll either contact me or, if I contact him first, he'll respond to my email. Still, I had to write something, and, unlike others who clearly felt the same way about the question, I didn't want to write anything sarcastic because I'm not a sarcastic person. The reality, of course, was: Who's not going to contact me because he doesn't think he's kind or respectful or communicates openly? Who actually thinks he's dumb, humorless, down on life, unfit, and pessimistic–even if he really is?)

Then, it was on to the fill-in-the-blanks, with a choice of responses regarding gender, ethnicity, education, smoking habits, drinking habits, marital status, occupation, hair color, eye color, political view, whether or not my children–if any–lived at home, how often I attended synagogue, and my body type. I had to fill in my height, my weight, where I grew up, and the desired age range of my "Ideal Match." From multiple answers, I had to choose (as many as I thought applied in each category) my favorite cuisines, music, pets, physical activities, pastimes. From there, I had to choose the acceptable marital status, religious background, education level, drinking habits, and smoking habits of my "Ideal Match."

Right at the top of the profile, next to my primary photo, I had to put a number to the left of the word, "Age." There was not enough space to put, "Sorry, that number is unlisted." It wasn't that I was ashamed of my age; it was just that under these circumstances . . .

This was my dilemma. Should I tell the truth? Yikes, I was three months shy of 60. Should I lie? After all, I really wanted to find a man in his mid-50s. And, really, I didn't look 60. Or feel it.

Or, I hoped, act it. But I'm not a liar. In fact, I pride myself on telling the truth. Still, I was certain, deep inside my gut, that choosing any two-digit number that starts with a six would be the kiss of death. It would fall outside the search parameters of the very men I was interested in. I couldn't possibly let that happen.

So, I lied. I said I was 57. But, I decided, it really wouldn't 'count' if I stuck to the following rule: I'd tell the truth about my age right away. Right away meant at the first meeting. Or before, if necessary, in an early email or phone conversation, but only if the question came up. As in, "How old are you *really?*" Trust me, I was asked. Especially by men who had been burned too many times before. These were the men who had met women who had said they were 59 years old, but turned out to be 70. Yes, it really happened. And the photos they posted were 11 years old. Or more.

I also lied about my marital status.

I was legally separated, but I chose "divorced." I had the sense that there aren't too many men who want to date a legally-separated woman. That's because most men think that a legally-separated woman is

a) still carrying the torch for her husband (and that could be true);

b) too new out of her marriage and shouldn't be dating yet (and that could be true);

c) in the throes of a contentious divorce and he could become implicated in the divorce proceedings, or worse (and that could be true).

But none of those applied to me, so it was better, I decided, to lie. Again, my rule applied. I would let a man know my true marital status as soon as we met, or before, if the subject came up. It did. But not as frequently as the subject of age. I could tell an online dating veteran by the generic question he would ask, usually during the initial phone conversation: "So, tell me what you lied about on your profile."

I lied about my drinking habits.

I chose social drinker when, in fact, I don't drink at all. When I wrote my first profile for jdate.com, I told the truth, but only for a brief period of time. I started lying when men started asking me whether I belonged to Alcoholics Anonymous. I worried that men were taking a pass on pursuing me because they assumed I had a drinking problem. (I didn't – and don't; I simply don't like the taste of alcohol.)

I lied about my geographic location.

I was living in a small community on the North Shore of Massachusetts, and I felt that men who saw my profile would think that I lived too far away from the greater Boston area. Or they would never even see my profile because I would fall outside their searches, based on their geographic parameters. So I lied and wrote that I lived in Boston. I knew that I loved going into Boston, so driving into the city wouldn't be a problem. It was not about, "I'll meet you half-way." If I indicated that I lived in Boston, then I had to be willing to drive to Boston. It worked.

I thought about lying about – or at least not mentioning – my educational background. I knew that there were men out there who were intimidated by a woman with a PhD. But I was proud of it, so I included it, then tempered it with, "More important than my degree was the education I received from life's experiences."

When I decided to switch to Match.com. I was attracted to the site not only because I had a broader religious base of men to choose from, but also because I was a lot less restricted in the way I could write my profile.

Now, you might be wondering, why would I care so much about writing the perfect profile if what I said in the previous chapter is true – that men only care about the photos? Maybe it's about my pride, my work ethic. After all, I saw finding a man online as my second career; I needed to take it seriously, work hard at it, be conscientious. And maybe I was looking for the exception to the rule – the man who did care about what I said about myself – after he looked at (and liked) my photos, of course.

There was something else: A "how-to-write-a-profile" epiphany. I had gone into jdate.com with no prior online dating experience. I had written my profile as a neophyte. Now, it was different. I had been a student for three-quarters of a year at the Dating School of Hard Knocks. What had I learned? Perhaps the most important lesson was that writing a profile is just like marketing a product. A profile is nothing more or less than a print advertisement designed to sell a product (in this case, me) to an audience (in this case, men). So, the question was, once my audience liked the packaging, would it buy the product? Or at least, sample it? Plus, as with any product, it's more than just writing a good ad. It's also about the competition, and, in this market of online dating, there's a lot of that out there. So just like any good marketing person, I needed to know as much as I could about those other "products." That was easy to determine. All I had to do was a search of the hundreds of women on Match.com who fell within my age and geographic range.

Trying to think like a man, I looked at the photos first. Whenever I saw a photo of a good-looking (in my opinion) woman, I opened her profile and read it carefully. I found that, with few exceptions, they were all saying the same thing:

I'm funny, intelligent, caring, giving . . . I'm looking for someone who's funny, intelligent, caring, giving.

Well, so was I. So, I wondered, how was I going to compete?

Answer: I needed to be perceived as different, and, hopefully, better.

I promised myself that I wasn't going to post a profile until it was different, and, hopefully, better. I worked on it. I worked on it. I worked on it, until . . .

I came up with the following:

Time to put on your thinking cap, and answer the following Multiple Choice and True-False questions.

1) *You see the glass*
   (a) half full
   (b) half empty
   (c) You can't see the glass

2) *You think*
   (a) out of the box
   (b) inside the box
   (c) What box?

3) *If you were chronologically younger, you'd want to date*
   (a) Carrie
   (b) Big
   (c) Charlotte

4) *You like to travel*
   (a) As often as you can
   (b) all the time because you have nothing else to do
   (c) never

5) *Your ex-spouse is*
   (a) still a good friend
   (b) someone you were once married to
   (c) the devil incarnate

True or false?

6) *Gender equality means he takes out the garbage; she cooks.*

7) *Women really like men to go shopping with them.*

8) *Two people who really care about each other have to be together 24/7.*

9) *Being in a relationship requires hard work.*

10) *Channel surfing is fun.*

How did you do? If you answered (a) to questions 1–5 and false to questions 6–10, please email me ASAP. After all, two half-full glasses make one full glass.

Different, eh? Clever, too?

I'm not even sure how I came up with the "test" idea. Was it the ex-school teacher in me? Or was it the realization that a test-as-profile could turn the tables–in a unique way? After all, I reasoned, don't men like to talk about themselves? This test would be a way to make my profile all about them, instead of about me. And because it was interactive, it would hopefully get them to look beyond my photos. If they were clever enough, intelligent enough (and wasn't that what I was looking for?), they would get 'it.' They would get 'me.' They could–would–appreciate who I was. And, it would follow, wouldn't it, that they would be who I was looking for.

Yes, the glass is full.

Once I had the profile written, the "tag line" came easy:

THIS IS ONLY A TEST

I liked that a lot. After all, what was a profile–no, what was this whole online dating scene–if it wasn't "only a test?"

All that was left was to come up with my online name. I had called myself DJK123 for jdate.com. How 'ho-hum' is that? I had promised myself that I wasn't going to be that boring ever again. Wanting to be perceived as different and clever meant that I had to have a clever name, too.

A friend of mine suggested that I incorporate Bond Girl in my name because, he said, "You remind me of a Bond Girl. How about THE WORLD'S OLDEST BOND GIRL?" No way! I'd kill myself before I'd refer to myself as "oldest" anything. And anyway, I had doubts about even calling myself a Bond Girl. After all, there was Pussy Galore, and I wasn't sure that associating myself with a Pussy sent the right message, at least not to the type of man I thought I was looking for.

I pushed for more information from my friend.

"A Bond Girl is exciting, adventurous, full of fun, and that's how I see you," he told me. "That's how I think men should think of you."

I ended up with:

ABONDGIRL4EVER

Did it work? On the face of it, I suppose, it did. Men seemed to like the name as much as the profile. I got a lot of positive feedback, and I felt that the men who responded were not "Average Joes." What I would ultimately discover was that it wasn't about whether the men actually took the test. In fact, the men who actually answered the questions—and especially those who told me their scores—turned out to be men that I didn't want to meet. When I tried to figure out why, I came up with the following possibility: They took my test a tad too literally, and I realized that I was not attracted to literal thinkers. It was the men who simply wrote, "Your profile was great (clever, funny, *whatever*)" that I wanted to meet. And usually did.

I met lots of men and went out with a handful of them more than once. But I hadn't even come close to finding The Right One. I needed to figure out why.

Was my profile too obtuse? Maybe it wasn't saying who I really was (beyond funny, intelligent, and clever) or what I really wanted. *Really* wanted? Did I really even know what I really wanted? Or was what I wanted when I wrote the profile not what I wanted anymore? And was that because I really didn't want it anymore, or because I was realizing that I couldn't get it? My head was swimming with questions.

When my Match.com six-month membership ran out, I didn't renew it. Instead, I promised myself that I wouldn't go back online until I came up with an entirely new profile. The only way I could do that was by figuring out who I really was and what I really wanted, or thought I could find, in a man.

Writing my second Match.com profile proved harder for me than the first because I decided I needed to discard "over-the-top clever." This time my profile needed to have an entirely different tone. I had reinvented myself, or so I thought. Now, the tenor of my profile had to reflect it. I made a list of how I thought it had to be:

Serious, determined, provocative, shocking, straightforward, totally honest (except about my age).

I believed, though, that the focus still had to be on what the man I was looking for had to have. Not who I was.

At one point I actually thought it was about money and control. I had met a man on Match.com, and I thought he had the right idea. He paid for everything and because he paid for everything, he could be in total control, or at least that's how it appeared to me. Well, I thought to myself, I can afford to pay for everything. So, if I pay for everything, will that give me the control I'm looking for? I actually wrote a profile that, I thought, would spell it out. No holds barred:

Are you a man who is willing to be financially supported by an independent (emotionally and financially) woman who wants companionship (specifics to be mutually agreed-upon) and is willing to pay for it? I want someone who will travel with me, eat meals with me (if you like to cook, you get bonus points; if you're actually good at it, you get more bonus points), and participate in other activities—some menial (be forewarned) like taking my car in for servicing, some negotiable (for example, taking yoga classes with me. If you already do yoga, add more bonus points). You are either retired or have a flexible job, so that traveling isn't a problem. You have interests of your own, are independent, and like your own space. You are intelligent, but not too intellectual, and you're very funny in a witty sort of way. You're sophisticated, but not stuffy, and you won't make a fool out of yourself in public or private, though a little quirky is good. You have lived a fulfilling life and still do. You don't have any axes to grind. You've already had a relationship with the love of your life; you don't need to find another "soul mate." You're physically fit, do not play golf or like to hike or kayak. You are, currently, at least 5'10". Please note: I'm definitely not desperate, nor am I looking for gold diggers or slugs.

I mulled over it for over a month, uncertain enough about its content to hold back from posting it while I tried to come up with other ideas. I came up empty. I needed help. So, I phoned Gary, my oldest, closest male friend who just happens to be a marketing expert in New York City. I told him I was coming to visit him, and the primary goal of my visit was to have him help me create a new profile.

"We'll brainstorm," I told him. The first thing I did was reiterate my vision for a new profile: Serious, determined, provocative, shocking, straightforward, totally honest (except about my age).

So far, so good. Then, I read him my "I want to be in control" profile. He was appalled. "We're starting from scratch," he said. "Give me a synopsis of the problem."

Oh, the problem! It was more than one. I took a deep breath and began:

No. 1: I hadn't met Mr. Right.

No. 2: I'd come to the conclusion that I wasn't going to meet Mr. Right, so why waste time 'advertising'?

No. 3: I'd decided that if I wasn't going to meet Mr. Right, I wanted to meet someone I could travel with. After all, I loved to travel, I had the time to travel and the money to travel, but I hated traveling alone, and I didn't have anyone, any man (I didn't really like traveling with women), to travel with.

I had always paid attention to how many men wrote in their profiles that they loved to travel. So, seeking a travel companion shouldn't be difficult, especially if I were straightforward about it. And being straightforward didn't–shouldn't–have to mean that I couldn't still show I was clever and intelligent and, even after all the online dating failures, still had a sense of humor.

I started talking it through and ended up with . . .

The following profile is meant to be serious, determined, and straightforward. It's the result of having been here before. Now, I'm going to try another way to communicate who I am and who I'm looking for.

The main thing I'm looking for is a traveling companion. I have been able to create a fortunate life for myself. My career, which I love, does not require my staying in one place. I spend part of my time in the Boston area, part of the time in South Florida, and my goal is to spend three to four months a year traveling, with at least two of those months in two foreign countries. But the truth is, I don't like traveling alone. I much prefer traveling with someone else, and I much prefer that someone else to be a male. Someone who is funny (yes, I know, everyone thinks they're funny. Funny here means you get my sense of humor; I get yours. No need to say, "I'm only kidding.") You're fun. You have stories to tell. You're upbeat. You don't sweat the small stuff. You're a problem-solver. You don't get angry. You're not highly analytical. You don't want to change a person. You don't compete (at least not with me, so that we can play Scrabble and it's OK if I win).

You have the time, the health, the incentive, and the interest to travel; you have the financial wherewithal (for your share) to travel. You're still involved in a career (one that you can take with you on trips) or you're retired but still have interests. You've traveled a lot already, and love to go back to your favorite spots (St. Barts? Vancouver? Amsterdam?), as well as discover entirely new places. You like to spend extended periods of time in one place, rather than hop from place to place. You don't like roughing it, but you don't require four-star hotels either. We'll enjoy doing things together, but we'll also relish times apart. (Often making for lively conversations over dinners.) Example: If you like museums and I like shopping, you can spend the afternoon at the museum; I'll spend it shopping. (No, I don't have to describe in detail what I bought over the steamed mussels.)

Need I say, this is not your garden-variety relationship? It's not about "one-and-only." (I've already had mine.) Or holding hands on the beach (though I don't rule that out). But first things first. Let's talk.

I was trying to convey a new identity, so I also decided to abandon ABONDGIRL4EVER. Surprisingly, it came to me as soon as I finished writing the profile.

IGOPLACES

The tagline came easy, too.

Come fly with me

That said it all. It commanded action on the part of the reader. And maybe it was about my being in control, as well. I wasn't going to fly with him; he was going to fly with me. I definitely liked that notion.

*N*ow, continue to the next chapter, or flip this book over to page 15 to see how you can do it, too.

CHAPTER FOUR

Trolling For Men:
How I Did It

STEP ONE: THE SEARCH

It all starts with checking out men's profiles. I can still remember the excitement I felt when I realized that all I had to do was choose an age range and mileage parameters, and a whopping 500 men would pop up for my consideration. Five hundred men. Now, that's incredible.

It was an even more heady feeling that just as I was trolling for men, they were trolling for me. In three years, over 3,000 men had looked at my profile. Three thousand-plus men. Now, that's mind-boggling.

My goal was to explore as broad a base as possible. I usually chose a 10-year age range (55–65, though if I got desperate, I'd go up to 67 or 68). I usually chose a 60-mile radius (though sometimes when I was desperate, I'd go up to 100 miles or even different states). I would not eliminate men by key words (e.g., leaving out men with no photos or men who had never been married, even though I rarely would consider those men). But sometimes (usually when I had nothing better to do), I would search key words like "Gemini," even though I wasn't really into astrology. And "yoga," even though most of the men who said they did yoga really didn't, or at least they hadn't in 20 years. So, why did they say it?

"Women are into men who put that in their profile," one man told me. "It makes them think we've tapped into our feminine side."

Next.

I was definitely not interested in that man.

In the beginning, it would take me four hours to work my way through the maze of photos and bravado. The more I did it, the better I became at speeding up the process.

Next.

Next.

It was so easy to move on to the next profile.

Soon, I was getting through 500 profiles in half the time. In part, of course, the speed was due to the fact that there were a lot of the same profiles popping up every time I did a search.

"Been there, seen him."

Next.

In part, it was because I was becoming savvier about how the system worked. For example, people on Match.com who don't want their profiles seen have to either manually "hide" them if their memberships haven't expired or specifically request that their profiles be removed if their memberships have expired. (Match.com and, I suspect, a lot, if not all, of the other dating sites, don't automatically remove profiles of elapsed or cancelled members. I suspect the reason is that it makes it look as though the site has more members than it actually has at any given time.) So, if I saw that a man hadn't logged on for "over three weeks," I took it as a sign that he was involved with someone or no longer a member.

Next.

I also became efficient, and proficient, at honing in right up-front on what I needed/wanted to find out that would determine the eligibility criteria I had established for myself. That's the beauty of online dating, of course. I could eliminate men without ever having to meet them. All I had to do was pay attention to what they wrote. My "deal breakers" were looking me straight in the eye.

Oh yes, my "deal breakers." What time-savers they were! I had learned this term early on from the men I met. When I first heard the phrase, I laughed out loud. What a macho/business-type expression being used about social relationships! Who did these men think they were? Donald Trump on dates? It got me thinking. At the end of an unsuccessful first meeting, maybe I could glare at the guy and exclaim, "You're fired!"

I carefully drew up my list of deal breakers:

If someone lived with his parents . . .
Next.
If someone had a roommate . . .
Next.
If someone had a kid, or kids, who lived at home, even "sometimes" . . .
Next.
If someone was a smoker, including – especially – anyone who said he was trying to quit . . .
Next.
If someone loved to play golf. Or hiked. Or kayaked. Or skied . . .
Next.
If someone loved to spend time with his grandkids . . .
Next.
If someone's profile was extremely negative . . .
Next.
Or too sarcastic . . .
Next.
If someone didn't have a college degree . . .
Next.

(It wasn't because I thought a man without a college degree wasn't intelligent; it was that a lot of men without a college degree—and even some with 'only' a bachelor's degree—were typically intimidated by my advanced degree. How did I know? They would say so. Of course, there were exceptions. I did go out with one man with an associate's degree, and I will never regret it. He's way more intelligent than I am, and he became—still is—a close friend. He has enhanced my life with his knowledge and his kindness.)

If someone's profile was poorly written . . .

Next.

(It wasn't just that I thought that poor spellers and poor grammarians weren't as bright as I was looking for, but reading between the lines, I wondered how much time they spent putting their profile together. In other words, how much did they really care? How much did they care about the impression they made on others? If they didn't care enough to even check their spelling, then how much did they care about themselves? How much were they going to care about me? If they didn't take the time to write a good profile, how serious were they about finding someone?)

If someone had never been married . . .

Next.

(I did make a couple of exceptions, because of specific attributes. The man who had never been married but who liked to dance and travel and did some real estate, for example; it didn't work out. He acted like a man who had never been married; he was way too set in his ways. Of course, I met a lot of divorced men who were way too set in their ways. And one of my never-married exceptions became—still is—a close friend.)

If someone wasn't politically liberal . . .

Next.

My list proved to be a work-in-progress. The more men I met, the more deal breakers I added to it. Still, in the end, I realized that my list had functioned only as a framework, a crutch, that I could–and did–rely on all along the way. But ultimately, the list proved meaningless. When I met my "Mr. Right," deal breakers that I had sworn by for three years flew out the proverbial window.

Then there were the turn-offs. There's probably a fine line between turn-offs and deal breakers, but I still tried to make the distinction.

There were visual turn-offs.

The first, of course, was the absence of photos. I would typically not respond to anyone who didn't post any photos unless there was something compelling about his profile, and then I would always request a photo. I remember only a couple of men acquiescing to my request, and once I received their photos . . .

"Oh, so that's why they didn't post a photo."

Next.

But, like most women–and unlike most men–the photos weren't that important to me in terms of great looks. In fact, I usually thought–and I was usually right–that if a man looked too good, it was probably a very old photo.

What was important to me was what the photos "said" about the man. I looked for smiles, eye contact with the camera, a twinkle in an eye. I was turned off by men who showed themselves with a bottle of beer; a glass of wine; another woman, even their adult daughter; a grandchild; a dog, especially a small one; a car, boat, plane, motorcycle, especially if they were pretending to be the owners; sunglasses; motorcycle goggles; baseball caps, especially with the brim turned backward; their shirts off.

I'd pay attention to the names men chose for themselves. I appreciated clever. And funny. And what it told me about them right off the bat.

Some of the names I liked were:

MusicUnitesUs
OneManAmongMany
Ironchefwannabe
PolandRomanski
Veritassquared

I'd pay attention to the taglines. Two of my favorites:

"If I can cook you a great meal, make you feel like Ginger Rogers on the dance floor, and induce a laugh regularly, can love be far behind?"

And,

". . . and so you got tossed from your pony. Brush it off and get back on. Life's too short to be taken out of the race over a little scuff."

And of course, I paid the closest attention to the text.

I was turned off by men who wrote that they liked to walk hand-in-hand on the beach (too needy). Or that they were looking for their "soul mate" (too unrealistic).

After going out with a handful of them, I typically would not respond to men who were retired, especially if they didn't sound like they had a life.

"So, what did you do today?" I would ask when they called.

"Oh, I took a walk, read the *New York Times*, made myself a tuna fish sandwich, took a nap. What about you?"

It wasn't just what a man said in his profile, but how he said it. Was there a style to his writing? I was always impressed when there was. Not only because he was capable of it, but because he took the time to show it. I always assumed that a man who took the time to write a stylish profile cared about the impression he was making, and took the time to make a good one.

Like the man who wrote under "Favorite Hot Spots":

Have you been to Dubrovnik? I've lived there and worked there. I love Italy, especially Venice and Sienna—who wouldn't? And closer to home, the Four Corners and Santa Fe are magical.

The same person wrote under "Favorite Things":

Lazy Sunday buckwheat pancake breakfasts.

Here's another profile I liked because it was so succinct. I imagined the author would not be long-winded like so many of the men I was meeting; that he really knew himself. I liked his sense of humor. Even better, it seemed to be 'my' sense of humor. This was an excellent example of someone who didn't have to say that he had a sense of humor; he showed it.

I'm extremely low maintenance, an excellent cook, have no bad habits, enjoy talking (even about emotions), and I'm reasonably housebroken. I'm warm, compassionate, funny, stable, resilient, and am looking to hopefully find some of those qualities in a partner. Not only am I willing to do odd jobs around the house and in the garden, but I actually enjoy them. My known weaknesses are: watching too much educational TV, needing a spell checker to write, and I can't sing.

Succinct isn't easy, so I was impressed with this one at only 71 words:

Independent-thinking, sure of my values. Thrown by the complexity of our lives: Hey! What do we make of this . . . Good at the big thought. Kind of abstract, but moved by the light touch and a smile. Interested in the wider landscape but most attentive to those important to me. Can remain quiet, gathering up the bits of thought that I spring on you to make you laugh, dispute, and amaze.

And this one which is exactly 70 words:

I invest money for people when I am not pondering life or exploring the edges of my universe. I strive to find balance in my life while continually growing and changing. I am successful, well-educated and feel that I am physically and emotionally at my best. I am looking for a special woman to play with, dance with and be intimate with on our journeys toward the mountain top.

I always paid close attention to how a man showed his sense of humor:

I'd quit golf if I didn't have so many nice shirts.

Or,

Will go practically anywhere, and can be talked into the rest of the places, with the notable exception of theme parks, a Jim Carrey movie, and The Jerry Springer Show.

I liked it when men turned a negative into a positive:

I don't like to dwell on all the bad news in newspapers and TV. Don't get me wrong, I do know what is going on in the world!

Then there were profiles that resonated for me personally:

I would prefer someone who likes to move to her own drummer, which may be anything from her unique style of dress to her own well-defined interests.

And,

I'm looking for a woman with stories to tell and stories yet to live out.

OK, so he was holding a bottle of beer in his hand in his main photo, and his age range was 47–57, but he wanted to learn the tango and how to swing dance, and he also wrote,

I am open to new things I normally might not think of, or think I would not like, if it is important to someone.

If I were to pick a favorite profile, it would probably be the following. To show why I liked it so much, I've deconstructed it (see my numbered notes below):

*The phone rang unexpectedly (1). Would I be interested in a terrific pro-
fessional opportunity in the Boston area (2)? A chance to be near my son, who
recently moved here (3). So I traded the wings for steamers and Molson's for
Sam Adams. I'm teaching Duffy to 'bahk' (4). But being the social person that
I am, it is vital to develop new friendships. If something more than friendship
happens here, I am VERY open to that (and I am confident that I would be
an excellent partner) (5). I consider myself an immensely flawed man hoping
to find someone slightly less flawed. I have done my work and consider myself
emotionally and spiritually strong (6). Unlike 98% of the profiles I have read,
I look and feel my age; and I say that with a touch of pride. I have lived every
one of my years—many moments with the greatest joy as well as my share of
pain (7). You will find me well-educated and traveled, and I do my share of
reading. My travels have taught me much more than my formal degrees. Although I am a card carrying capitalist, I would rather discuss matters spiritual
or metaphysical. While I am Catholic, I respect and value all religious beliefs
and am a champion of human rights, non-violence, the poor, and respect for
all living things. I am financially stable and value security more than material-
ism. My politics have a definite list to port; I am quite disturbed and saddened
by events in the world—and the direction of this country (8). I am competent
in the kitchen and on the dance floor, and I am pretty good at Scrabble (9). I
sometimes think I suffer from the Peter Pan syndrome (growing old is manda-
tory; growing up is optional) (10). If any of these appeals to you, perhaps you
would join me for coffee, a drink, or even sharing a meal (11).*

(1) What a wonderful—and totally unique—way to start a profile. Like "Once upon a time," it makes you want to read on, to get
to the happy ending!

(2) Ah, he's a professional, and he's on-the-ball, too, if at this
stage in his life, he's getting "terrific" opportunities. Most men I
met complained about their jobs. Many had been laid off from
good jobs they were trained to do and now had to become used car
salesmen, or ferry boat captains, or worse. Or they were counting
down to retirement.

(3) He has a family that he cares about, a son who doesn't live
at home, not even sometimes.

(4) He obviously wants someone who can think on her feet – and knows her geography and beer. And he has a sense of humor!

(5) Now, here's a guy who's not going to jump into bed with you on the first date. (Unless YOU want him to?)

(6) Humble about his accomplishments? That's a nice trait.

(7) Now, that's unique and thoughtful. Note how he's paid attention to other profiles.

(8) What a wonderful way of covering important topics that most people don't even address in their profiles. And doesn't he make you feel as though he'll listen to opposing points of view? Doesn't he convey a sense of caring and kindness?

(9) Nice segue into the more mundane, but equally important and intriguing, especially for us Scrabble players. (Don't you bet he's better than pretty good at Scrabble? But he'll let you win the first time?)

(10) If he had asked me to edit his profile, I probably would have told him to take this out. It seems to contradict his look-and-feel-his-age comment.

(11) Isn't this a really nice way to end a profile? How could someone turn down an offer like that?

There was not one spelling mistake. Excellent use of semi-colons. Commas in just the right places. Ease with sophisticated grammatical structure. And didn't he totally convey a personality here vs. a list of wants and don't-wants?

Unfortunately, there were more profiles that turned me off than turned me on.

I equated too much intensity in a profile with being needy. In the following profile, I sensed a man who was not only needy but also egocentric and controlling:

I want our moments to be the deep water . . . I'm not so interested in facts—I'm interested in you.

I looked for what appeared to be openness and honesty, but I was turned off by too much—and certain types of—sexual reference. For example:

When we're immersed in sensuality, you're as excited about my pleasure as I am about yours, and we always try to take it further, to experiment, heighten everything. I encourage your explorations and your experiences, wherever they lead you. I am not and never will be jealous.

Or,

I am a very creative and imaginative lover outside the vanilla world. I seek a woman who is free and playful in and out of the bedroom, curious, open, and exploratory.

I was turned off by men who turned "Favorite Hot Spots," into sexual innuendos too.

Here's an example:

Hmmm, favorite 'hot spots'? Ahhh, that's easy . . . my ears and neck!!

Still, there were profiles that put sex "out there," but in a way that worked for me:

. . . When you connect with someone it's immediate, intense, and on multiple levels—mental, emotional, spiritual, and sexual. You try to enjoy love, avoid the urge to control it, and just see where it takes you. Physical chemistry is the key part of the initial spark for you. Although people love to talk about sex, the truth is that most people are afraid of their 'wild' side. You aren't. You trust your instincts and know exactly who you find attractive and what turns you on. That said, your approach to love can change over time. Physical passion may become less crucial and commitment will become more important.

Here's a profile that turned me off (right down to missing punctuation and errors in spelling, capitalization, and syntax):

When I first started with Match, I felt like a little boy in a candy store. Now, after numerous introductions or should I say interviews, I fell more like a Human Resource manager for a Fortune 500 company! I'm really not interested in how many degrees you have, the size of your stock portfolio, or how you broke through the 'glass ceiling'. I am interested in how I weaken your knees when I hold you, accelerate your heartbeat when you think of me, and that you are able and willing to express and share those type of emotions with me naturally. Let's not make this anymore complicated than it already is. After all, I'm sure we've all had our share of heartaches at this point of our lives. So, if you are at least mildly attracted to my photo, have a PERSONALITY, understand the meaning of chemistry, and aren't too concerned that we don't 100% match this sites compatibility guidelines, it's quite ok to continue . . .

I'm assuming this brief intro should give you a bit of insight into my basic personality, and thank you for not moving on to the next profile just yet. Let's see if you can stay with me as I continue to simplify and define some other fundamental personal traits and appealing characteristics. Here are some easy questions that should help with your intuitive sense of judgment and attraction. Are you willing to kiss on the first date if the mood should strike you? Are you relatively spontaneous and open-minded? Must I love your dog or cat before I love you? Do you prefer to walk down a busy city street at noon, or barefoot on a sandy beach at midnight? Have you ever made love in the woods? Does children's laughter still bring a smile to your face? Do you mind getting your hair tossed in a convertible? Have you given up on wearing form-fitting jeans? Are you sensitive, caring, compassionate, playful, romantic, affectionate, and expressive? Are you still reading this profile? Hmmmm, still here, huh? Gee, what a fine judge of character you must be!

Really, I just wanted to smack him! My reaction was: This man is controlling, sarcastic, narcissistic, hostile, and will push for sex on the first date. I could have been all wrong, but I wasn't going to bother checking it out. I operated with my gut when I read profiles, and I always trusted my gut.

I was turned off by:

The men who tell you what you should do:

You should be wanting to be worshipped and adored 24/7. When we go out, you should expect me to open the doors for you, and hold your hand wherever we go. You should also expect me to look lovingly into your eyes and tell you often how beautiful you look. (That will be the most important job I can have, your beauty consultant.)

The narcissists:

Looking for a lady that knows how to make a man feel like a man and wants to make him happy.

The men who didn't seem to think it was important to update their profiles. (I was certain that this was a sign that their photos were outdated, too.) As in,

Hopelessly addicted to the Red Sox; maybe I am not as good a learner as I'd like to think. (Clearly, this man hadn't updated his profile since 2003.)

If I had to pick what I thought was the worst profile to cross my screen, I'd pick this one, exactly as it was written by a 52-year-old seeking women 29–73. Anywhere in the United States.

Well . . . I am an easy going love to cook keep a neat place romantic sexy out going good lisener open to any situation honest no room for sadness happyness is all good good provider love children and pets are cool Ansd I need some one that be a lady in front of my friends and family one that will enjoy cooking with me. An sexy romantic in the bedroom truly looking for some one to be my equal partner in life one that will be her self and try not to change one to the other but to be one and grow to be ONE in good and strong spirit to be honest and respect each other as I will do the same and be supportive in my woman decisions in life and help her as she will do the same . . . stay cool and hope to hear from you soon. So, this is all I needed in a woman and I want to spend the rest of my life with such a woman and will do anything for her in other to make her happy. I dont like games, and I am not a game player aswell . . . so lets just be honest with each other and see what happens between the both of us. Baby, I want to love and to beloved again, cause it has been long now and I will never break a womans heart. My ex sleept with my best friend and now

I dont have trust in my friends. I am all alone and just want it that way and I like it that way. Well . . . I have an accent, as I was born and brought up in London, have only lived in usa for about 35 years. I am a building contractor . . . I love you.

How did I even stumble on his profile? He sent me a "form" email in which he said that he was "looking for an honest lady . . ." I guess that's what must have attracted him to my profile!

But honestly, through it all, I enjoyed the process. I loved reading profiles. I loved to analyze them, read between the lines, laugh out loud, make comments out loud (often obscene). It was totally entertaining, and – I can't deny it – it gave me something to do in my spare time when there was nothing to watch on TV, I was home alone, and lonely. But even when it was recreational, it was always serious and purposeful. It was a job that required that I meet as many men, who fit within my parameters, as quickly as I could.

I developed a system when I did my searches. I'd write down the names of the men I thought I was interested in pursuing, and once I got through all of them, I'd go back to the interesting ones and re-read their profiles. If I was still interested, I'd send them an email. On a typically fruitful search, it could be as many as 50.

STEP TWO: THE INITIAL CONTACT

I knew instinctively that I couldn't sit back and wait for men to contact me. And my instincts were correct. Most men, especially those of a "certain" age, don't need to contact women. They can just sit back and wait for the women to contact them. As a rule, then, I found that the men who did contact me were not men I wanted to meet. Plus, because I liked being in control, it certainly felt like I was in more control when I contacted the men first.

I kept my emails short, but sweet. Long emails were simply not time-efficient or necessary. When I received a long email, I would wonder, "Does this man have too much time on his hands?" It didn't make a good impression.

I wouldn't say anything about myself in my email. I shouldn't have to. A good profile says it all. So instead, I would shower the recipient with flattery. I had a simple and straightforward format.

The heading:

Wow!

The text:

I just read your profile, and I liked (was intrigued by; was blown away by; loved) not only what you said but how you said it. I hope you enjoy my profile as much as I enjoyed yours. My name is . . .

Dale

If there really was something that stood out, especially something that we had in common, I'd allude to it.

Then, I would wait.

STEP THREE: HOPEFULLY, THE RESPONSE

As a rule, I would get responses from about half of the men I wrote to. Positive responses, that is. Sometimes, men would send a "thanks, but no thanks" email. Often, it was a canned–prepared–response that the site provided. I found it totally unnecessary, insulting, a colossal waste of time for both the sender and for me, and often disappointing, especially if I had been very turned on to that person's profile.

An email from _____! I'd get excited. "He wrote back; he wrote back!" And then I'd open it. He's not interested. How depressing is that!

It wasn't like I needed an "I'm not interested" email to know that someone wasn't interested. As far as I was concerned, the absence of a response was a very clear message. That was all I needed. (I rarely sent "not interested" emails either, unless there was something about the person's email that I wanted to comment on — in a positive way.)

It was not unusual to receive a "Yes, I'm interested" email response, but there would be something about it that turned me off. Sometimes the turn-offs were so subtle, I just had a gut reaction to them — and trusted my gut. No need to figure out why. Sometimes the turn-offs were obvious. As in,

You're hot!

Or worse:

Your hot!!!!

I was turned off by men who wanted to engage in extended email correspondence. In the beginning, I fell for it — until I realized that these men were looking for an email "pen pal," and, for whatever reason (they were married, relationship-phobic, under house arrest), would never come around to actually meeting. As a result, I had a rule: No more than four emails, preferably two or three. As in, I sent the initial email; he responded and hopefully, he included his phone number and/or asked for mine. Even if he didn't and I liked his email response enough to write back, I would be totally direct:

Thanks for writing back. Please call me so we can arrange a time to get together. My cell phone number is: _____.

Like the men who wanted to be my "pen pals," there were men who wanted to become my "phone buddies." No thank you. I have better things to do with my time. Like search online for other men. If a man couldn't commit to a time and place to meet in two phone conversations or less, it was "Bye-bye Phoneman."

I didn't automatically go out with any man just because we made it to the phone call phase. It was not unusual for a man to make a dreadful impression over the phone. In those situations, I would be honest. "I've enjoyed this phone conversation, but I think I'm going to pass on our getting together."

Next.

Of course, there were no guarantees that a man who made a good impression on the phone would make a good impression in person. The proof was in the meeting.

STEP FOUR: THE MEETING

What was once called "the first date" has become, in the jargon of online dating, "the meeting." (The next get-together is "the first date.")

I can't think of any other experience that provokes such emotional extremes as the meeting.

On the one hand, there's the excitement:

I'm going to meet someone new.

On the other hand, there's the dread:

I'm going to meet someone new.

On the one hand, there's the giddiness around preparing for "the meeting."

What should I wear?

On the other hand, there's the trepidation:

What if I trip in these high heels?
What if my deodorant fails me?
Does my hair look OK?
What if he's loud and obnoxious, ugly as sin, a real jerk?
What if he doesn't like me?

I was petrified. But I tried to never let on. A couple of minutes ahead of time (five minutes if I was really nervous), I'd muster up all my yoga techniques: deep, steady breathing; positive, up-beat mantra ("I'll get through this" or "This will be fun" or "I'm psyched" or, in the worst case, "I can leave in an hour"); smile.

"Smile, smile, smile," I'd say to myself as I headed toward the meeting place.

And I did.

Please don't think I'm corny, but it always amazed me what that smile did for me – relaxed my face (which made my body relax); made me look positive (even if I wasn't feeling it) and upbeat. Some men told me that their first impression of me was "sparkly." That was a good thing.

When a man saw me smiling, it immediately made him smile, which, I contend, led to a good start. No guarantees, of course, that it would end well, but at least I felt as though I were giving it my all.

I'd look him straight in the eye, keep smiling (no matter what I was thinking), and extend my hand to shake his. (Sometimes he would take my hand, then lean toward me so that he could plant a kiss on my cheek. I reserved judgment on whether I considered it appropriate. In other words, if I liked his looks, I didn't mind.)

I usually let the man decide where we should meet. It was often Starbucks. For coffee. Later, it would dawn on me that I never went out with a man for a second time who had suggested Starbucks. For coffee. For the meeting. Maybe it was too uncreative, and too safe. I simply wasn't into safe, uncreative males. So, I wondered, had I listed Starbucks for coffee as one of my deal breakers, could I have saved myself a lot of time?

Even if it wasn't Starbucks, it was 'like' Starbucks – a place for coffee where the customer orders, pays, and picks up at the counter. It's not just about casual; the guy is pretty much guaranteed that it doesn't have to cost him any money. All he has to do is get there ahead of time and place/pay for his order. I'd find him at a table, waiting for me to join him. But first, I'd have to place/pay for/pick up my own cuppa joe.

You know, I really think that men thought that that was an original idea, and that I'd never catch on. It made a bad first impression on me. I thought it was rude (I preferred that a man waited for me outside, or just inside, our chosen destination. That's what I would do if I arrived first), and it said a lot about the person.

The alternative to coffee – meeting for drinks – made a lot of sense because if we were really getting along then, one of us – usually the man – could suggest that we extend drinks to dinner. But I often found going for drinks awkward because the potential rejection sort of hovered over us, or at least it hovered over me.

If I liked the guy, I would be thinking, "What if he doesn't suggest dinner?"

If I didn't like the guy, I would be thinking, "I hope he doesn't suggest dinner."

Meanwhile, the guy might be thinking, "I'd like to suggest dinner, but what if she says, 'No'?"

(Surprise: Men hate to be rejected! The more I met them, the more I realized that they weren't as thick-skinned or confident as I had imagined. They hated to have to make the first move.)

A handful of men would suggest dinner (and drinks) right off the bat. Usually, they were either new to the online dating scene (and therefore enthusiastic and upbeat), or they were very lonely.

The typical reason why a man suggested dinner for the meeting was, "I have to eat anyway."

I understood the logic. I hated eating alone, too.

But the risky part of dinner, of course, was it usually meant a longer time-commitment. That wasn't bad if I liked the person, but if I didn't like the person, it could feel like a life sentence.

With dinner, comes the question: Who pays? My rule was, I was always ready, willing, and able to pay my share, and I always offered. I was always able to pay the entire bill, should the occasion arise. Think: he excuses himself to go to the men's room, then slips out the door. It's happened (according to the men who say they've done it), but never to me.

Men also tell tales of it happening to them. Too much information? No, I encourage full disclosure. By the end of the meeting, I usually understood why the woman did it. Not that I think it's right. (I tried never to be rude. I never wanted to burn my bridges.) But I understood.

Though I never actually kept track, I would have to say that the majority of the men I met accepted my offer to contribute to the bill. I would acquiesce graciously if a man rejected my offer, but only if I knew I liked him enough to want to go out with him again. I would be more adamant about paying for myself if it was a man who, I was sure, I never wanted to see again. I felt that it was wrong for him to pay for me if I knew I wasn't interested in a future, even one more time, with him.

I always took note of the man who tallied up the check, then told me how much I owed, usually to the penny (tax and tip included) – unless he felt he was the one who spent more and therefore wanted to pay more. Pulling out a calculator (yes, it happened) was always the kiss of death.

Next.

Once I met a man who told me that if a woman didn't offer to pay, he'd pick up the bill, look it over, tally it up in his head, tell her what she owed, and never call her again – whether or not he had, up until that point, enjoyed her company. Later, I thought, I could have told him, "Perhaps you should ask for the check before the food comes out. Then, if she doesn't offer to pay her share, you can just cancel the order and leave!"

But, to be fair, there is another side. I hate to say it, but I strongly believe that women join online dating services for free meals, free movies, free concert and theater tickets. A lot of men believe this, too. The more women they meet, the more they develop – and practice – survival techniques.

Like the man from Match.com who suggested that we meet at a mall for an early dinner. He deserved an A+. Actually, it was even cleverer than simply saying, "Let's meet at the mall." He said, "Let's meet in front of Legal Sea Food," a very nice restaurant located at the mall.

He was there, waiting. I arrived, smiling. We shook hands. He smiled back, then said, "You know, I'm not really that hungry. Why don't we just grab a bite at the food court?"

Meaning: "Your looks don't turn me on enough to warrant a real restaurant commitment." Too much time; too much money.

In this case, I wasn't sorry. His looks hadn't turned me on either. Of course, one of us just could have said, "Uh, I don't think we're a match," and left. But hey, we both had to eat, and who wants to eat alone? We headed for the food court, got on separate lines. (See, we didn't even like the same cuisine.) In less than an hour, it was over, and I got to go shopping on a full stomach!

It always amazed me how quickly the "No Chemistry Here" lights went on, and how quickly I – or he – was ready to move on.

Next.

For me, the meeting was all about uncovering the deal breakers and turn-offs that don't appear on the profile. After all, is anyone going to write:

I'm argumentative.

Or maybe he really doesn't think he is. The point was, I thought so. But still, I sat through the 60 minutes, and I smiled. At least, I tried to.

And there were the turn-offs. Bad table manners, for example. But I've yet to see a profile in which the writer notes:

I have lousy table manners.

I had to find it out at the meeting. But still, I sat through the 60 minutes, and I smiled. At least, I tried to.

In retrospect, it's amazing what I sat through, what I listened to:

Men who dissed
their ex-wives,
their adult children,
their former bosses,
their kids' spouses,
their parents.

Men who still loved their mothers.

Men who told me
what I should order,
how to run my business,
how fabulous they were,
how fabulous they were in bed.

Men who wanted to
borrow money,
kiss my neck,
share an entrée.

Men who worried.

Men who didn't take chances.

Men who did all the talking.

Men who showed me pictures of their
grandchildren,
children,

pets,
yacht they had to sell to pay child support.

Men who complained.

Men who didn't laugh at my jokes.

Men whose jokes I didn't laugh at.

Men who were
cheap,
negative,
judgmental,
unethical,
unkempt,
hypochondriacs,
immature,
boring,
instantly familiar,
(still) in therapy,
racist,
homophobic,
gender-biased.

Men who
didn't look like their photos,
interrupted,
flirted with the server,
demeaned the server,
criticized,
bragged about themselves, especially about things they had
gotten away with,
had too much emotional baggage,
referred to women as girls.

Men who told
dirty jokes,

racist jokes,

gay jokes.

Men with medical and/or financial problems. (Looking for a nurse or a purse, or both?)

Men who didn't listen.

Men who repeated themselves.

Men who couldn't remember.

Men who answered their cell phones (except in rare, pre-warned situations, as in, "My father just had triple bypass surgery, and I may get a call from my mother.")

Men who made phone calls (except in rare, pre-warned situations).

Men who didn't make eye contact.

Men who gave themselves insulin shots right at the table.

Men who confessed to lies on their profiles that were on my list of deal breakers. (Smoking habits, as in, "I thought I would have quit by now." Marital status, as in "I'm still living with my wife, but we have an understanding." Those sorts of deal breakers.)

Men who lived with their parents.

Men who had a roommate.

Men who rented.

Men who watched more than two hours of television a night.

Men who got hotel rooms in Las Vegas for free.

Men who got drunk.

Trust me, it didn't take long to meet all of the above. But I kept smiling.

I asked lots of questions. No wonder men would say to me, "I feel like I've just been through an interview." (OK, sometimes they called it an interrogation!) Maybe it was my journalism background. Or maybe it was my need to know. And know quickly. I never saw any advantage to waiting.

The men I met seemed to like their role as "the interviewee." It's just their nature, I think. The ones who were more evolved, or at least thought they were, would often say to me, "I want to hear all about you," but, before I could say, "I graduated from . . ." they'd be saying, "Oh, that's interesting. I graduated from . . . , and then I . . ."

By the end of the hour-or-so (the typical length of initial time spent getting to know each other), I'd inevitably know a lot more about him than he knew about me. I found that worked to my advantage when I knew that I never wanted to see the guy again.

First, if I didn't want to see him again, I really didn't want him to know anything about me.

Second, I found it a lot easier to ask questions (and tune out during the answers) than to answer questions.

Third, it didn't take me long to get tired of hearing myself talk about myself during those first encounters. So, when I didn't have to, it was usually a relief. It was just a matter of being polite. Sometimes being polite wasn't that easy.

Here's an example of a really bad meeting when my politeness was really put to the test:

I stood in front of the restaurant looking forward to meeting the man with the very interesting profile and a wonderful sense of humor that made me laugh multiple times during our lively phone conversation. He and I had agreed to meet for dinner at a casual restaurant within walking distance of his apartment. I thought I knew the direction he would be coming from. As I looked up the street, I saw a man with a cane, bent over and walking at a snail's pace. He was the only person walking toward the restaurant. But how could this be the same person who had written that he was 56 years old and

 . . . *enjoy walking, hiking, camping, bike-riding, swimming, canoeing, swing dancing.*

"Dear God," I prayed. "Please don't let this be him." God must not have heard me.

I could have told him, when he introduced himself, that he was nothing like his profile, and headed for my car, but I didn't. I was hungry, and I suppose I was curious. I wanted to find out why he wrote what he wrote.

He told me that he had had cancer and the chemotherapy had damaged his back. But, he hoped, with time things would improve, and he would be able to do all the things he had written about. I expressed my disapproval, suggested that he change his profile, ate quickly, and got ready to leave. I was stunned when he asked me if I'd see him again. Had this man not heard a word I said?

"You gotta be kidding," I said, and left. So much for being polite.

So, imagine my surprise when I found an email from him waiting for me when I got home.

Hi Dale:

It was all my pleasure to be able to spend some time with you tonight. You are a beautiful, vibrant woman with eyes and a smile that can kill. I hope that I didn't disappoint you in your eagerness to find someone to travel with you, and I wish you good luck in your search. I just want to reiterate that I am not restricted in my activities because of my disability, and that includes traveling as well as everything else that comes with a lasting rela-tionship. However, I can't travel right now until they find the right mix of treatment so that I will feel much better. Also, as I'm sure you surmised, I can't financially support a life of all travel at this time . . . That doesn't mean that I won't, or that I'll never be able to travel with you. It only means that if we decide that we like each other more than anything, then I will begin to dedicate my savings to taking trips with you from time to time. If our lifestyles were exactly the same, it would be boring, wouldn't it? Differ-ence makes for excitement and permanence. I would like to get together with you again in between your trips, if that would please you. I had a great time tonight even though it was too short. I know that there must be much that I need to learn about you and I should have let you talk more about yourself. I hope that we will get that opportunity. Dale, I know that you must be such a sweetheart. I hope to hear from you again soon.

"You gotta be kidding," I said to myself, as I turned my computer off without responding. There was no way I wanted to see him again.

If I thought I wanted to see a man again, I made sure that I told him "My Story." Mine was a tell-all tale – the lies I had written in my profile; the skeletons in my closet.

I developed a "script." I knew how important it was to tell it well. I became masterful at setting the scene. It was usually easy.

Me: "So, what has your online dating experience been like?"

He: "You can't believe the number of times I've met women who don't look at all like their photos."

Me: "Is that because they've lied about their age."

He: "Yup."

Me: "Well, my photos are definitely recent, but I have to tell you . . . I lied about my age. I'm really ___. And while I'm at it . . . " That's when I would go down my list of lies. Get it over with.

Why did I tell all, right off the bat? Even when my friends told me that I should wait.

Answer: I felt that it was wrong to withhold information.

My friends protested. "Let him get to know you better," they told me. "If he knows you better, he'll be more accepting. He won't mind so much if you tell him after he really likes you as a person."

And I responded, "Bullshit. If they can't accept it right from the beginning, I'm not interested in them." Plus, I had heard stories from men about women waiting to tell them something – usually their real age – and the men turned on them, "What else are you keeping from me?" they would ask. "How do you expect me to trust you?" Well, some might think that was a tad extreme, but still . . .

I wasn't going to take any chances. Not after this early-in-my-online-dating-career experience:

We met for coffee, and I liked him. He was nice looking (for a man in his 60s). A retired doctor, he seemed intelligent. He was entertaining, too. A raconteur with a lot of humorous stories to tell, but nothing too personal. Even though I realized at the end of our meeting that I knew nothing more about him than I had read in his profile, I said, "Yes," when he asked me whether we could get together over the weekend, this time for dinner. He told me that he would pick me up; I told him I would meet him at the restaurant.

"I don't know where I'll be coming from," I told him. It was a lie, a necessary lie at a time when it was better than saying, "I never get into a man's car until I really get to know him." For me, it wasn't about fear for my personal safety (except if he were a lousy driver), but rather it was about my holding onto my independence, my need to be in control. With my own car, I could leave whenever I wanted to. If the date was a bomb, the last thing I wanted to do was have an awkward drive home with someone I never wanted to see again. Or vice versa.

But I was looking forward to this "first date." The very nice restaurant he had chosen was located in a very nice hotel. At the last minute, I decided to bring a toothbrush. Better safe than sorry, I said to myself, and chuckled.

We were seated at a banquette, so that we sat side-by-side instead of across from each other. Later, I would realize, it couldn't have been better. It meant that I could look straight ahead as he talked. I didn't have to make eye contact.

Right around the sixth shrimp in my cocktail appetizer, I realized that he was continuing where he had left off over coffee. He was entertaining me with his stories again. This time it wasn't going to be enough for me. I wanted to know about him.

"Tell me about yourself," I said.

I thought a broad-based question would work best. I was right. I had opened the flood gates. First, he bashed his ex-wife. Then, he started in about his daughter—a lesbian with an African-American girlfriend. He certainly had a lot to say about homosexuality (he was clearly homophobic) and about race (he was clearly racist).

I listened, and I ate. The more I listened, the faster I ate.

"So, what do you think?" he asked me when he had finished sharing his past and present with me.

"I think I have to leave," I said.

He didn't get it.

"What do you mean?" he said.

"I'll give you the *Reader's Digest* version," I told him, though I would have preferred to just leave. "I have a daughter, too. Her father is African-American. We were never married. The man I was married to was bisexual. He left me for a man."

As I had expected, he tried to right his wrongs.

"I really didn't mean . . . ," he began.

Saved by the server who came to clear our plates, and ask, "Would you care to see the dessert menu?"

"No. Just the check, please," I said.

When it came, I offered to pay my share.

He replied, "No, that's OK. Let me pay."

And even though I was breaking my rule, I let him.

We both left the table together, but he headed for the men's room, and I headed for my car.

There were a lot of other times when the meeting was great, but the next time – the first date – was a bomb. Like he sent his evil twin for the second encounter.

This was probably my worst experience:

He was a writer, so we had a lot in common and a lot to talk about. It had been such a promising meeting that lasted long enough to practically call it a first date. We had an early dinner, took a very pleasant walk, and agreed that we were looking forward to seeing each other again. He suggested a jazz cruise which sounded great to me. He insisted on making all of the plans. He would order the tickets, and he would pick me up. I was OK with the former, but not the latter. As always, I wanted to have my own car. After a mini-argument over it (not a good sign), he agreed that we would meet close to the destination, and he would call me with directions. But ultimately, when it came to the logistics, exactly where to meet, and what time, he seemed a little fuzzy on the details. He didn't know the actual name of the place he wanted us to meet – a parking lot on a main street – which was near the restaurant (he couldn't remember the name) that he thought we could eat at before heading for the dock to board the cruise. But he wasn't sure that we would grab something to eat first.

"You'll recognize the parking lot when you get there," he told me.

"Why don't I call you when I get there?" I offered.

He didn't have a cell phone.

I found it, or at least I thought I found it, and I was there on time. There were two possibilities, as far as I could tell, two parking lots a couple of blocks from each other. After waiting 15 minutes, I drove to the other parking lot and waited 15 minutes. Then, I returned to the first one. I made the same trip again, and just as I was certain that "This is a no-show," my phone rang. He had borrowed someone's cell phone. (Too cheap, it turned out, to call me from a pay phone.) I was pissed off. I waited for an apology for being late. No apology.

"He'll apologize when he sees me," I thought to myself. Wrong. That pissed me off even more.

There was no time to grab that bite to eat, especially since he wasn't sure where the dock was.

"Hop into my car," he suggested.

I don't think so.

"Come on," he cajoled. "We'll have to pass here on the way back."

"I'm going to take a different route home," I told him. It was a lie.

I followed him in my car for about 15 minutes. Suddenly, he pulled over to the side of the road and got out of his car. I knew why. He walked around the block to find someone who could give him directions. I thought for a moment or two, then turned my car around to face the other direction. I could have just left, I know, but I felt that would have been too rude. When he returned, he noticed that my car was facing in the opposite direction and walked over.

"Let's go," he told me.

"I'm not going," I replied.

"What's your problem?" he wanted to know. "Did you have a bad day."

What a jerk!

"I'm not going," I repeated.

"Then you owe me $16 for the ticket," he told me.

I gave him the money. That's the kind of person I am.

The next morning, there was an email from him, a poem of sorts, I suppose.

It read:

Dale, Dale,
You make me wail
If you were my woman, I'd jump on the third rail.

I couldn't resist. I wrote back:

Does that mean you want to see me again?!

*N*ow, continue to the next chapter, or flip this book over to page 31 to see how you can do it, too.

CHAPTER FIVE

What About Sex?
How I Did It

First, I did the math. I hadn't had sex with anyone other than my husband for three decades. How daunting was that? I couldn't possibly imagine standing naked in front of a virtual stranger. My body may have been good enough for a spouse of almost 25 years (plus the five years we dated), good enough on someone my chronological age, but would it pass muster with Mr. Right-Now? It wasn't just about exposing my naked body. It was about having my body touched by a stranger, and vice versa. I admit it; after being in the same bed with the same man for almost 30 years, I had settled quite comfortably into the missionary position. Now, it embarrassed me to even think of the alternatives. I also knew that I had become a little sloppy in the how-to-please-a-man department. Maybe I had even forgotten how.

The only positive spin I could come up with for myself was, I was lucky to be a woman. My sexual performance wouldn't be predicated on getting – and sustaining – an erection.

In fact, I had no idea whether the men-of-a-certain-age I would go out with would even be able to engage in sexual activity, and, well, I was certain that I could live with that. It might even be a relief. It was the relationship that would be important to me. I had had my fill of sex; sex was overrated. I didn't need it anymore. Certainly not at my age. Or so I thought at first.

It turned out I was wrong, on all counts!

Men who were online were definitely looking for relationships, sex included. And I found myself opening up to new possibilities and experiences, even some that I had feared. I was exposed to phone sex, sex toys, sexy underwear and lingerie, and sexual positions I had never imagined. I may have started out online comparing myself to Carrie on *Sex and the City*, but I discovered that in bed, I was really Samantha!

I felt younger, more vibrant, more creative, more in control, more exciting, more excited, and more enlightened, thanks to the men I slept with. But it wasn't just about the men I slept with; it was about how my definition of sex evolved. Sex no longer defined the relationship. It became a stand-alone act, something that I could enjoy wholeheartedly because there were no strings attached. I've never had such good sex. I've never felt so sexually liberated. I've never been so sexually satisfied. My body may not look like it did when I was 25, but I'm prouder now than I was then about its performance in bed.

That's probably why I would find myself – in bed – wondering, "Should I be searching for a younger man?" Like when I would whisper something insanely erotic into a man's ear, and he'd reply, "Speak up. I can't hear you."

Lesson learned: Always position yourself on the side of his good ear. If he has one. If he doesn't have one?

Next.

Just as I had thought about rules for all the other facets of my online dating career, I wondered what my rules about sex should be. It seemed to me that this was an area that required the most rules. After all, it was no longer just about when to have sex. It was about how to have sex. Between the time I had stopped dating and now, AIDS, and all the other STDs, had reared their ugly – and potentially fatal – heads. I no longer had to worry about birth control; my biological clock had stopped ticking years ago. Now, I had other equally, if not more, serious issues to think about. Now, it was about protecting myself against disease – and death. Condoms had become an answer to disease control.

I assumed that the men I'd engage in sexual intercourse with would have their own supply of condoms, but just in case, I purchased a box of Trojans (the only brand I knew) and put it in the drawer of my nightstand.

So, one night, in the throes of passion, when the first man I allowed into my bed whispered huskily, "Do you want me to use a condom?" I whispered back, "Yes. Yes."

He fumbled for it (he had brought his own), tried to get it on, lost his erection, rolled off of me, put his clothes on, and left.

It was then that I decided that my only rule about sex was that I would have no rules. If a man wanted to use a condom, he could – even though, I must admit, I personally enjoyed sex much more if the man didn't wear one. It turned out to be a non-issue, really. Only one man I slept with used a condom!

I don't know how to say this delicately or diplomatically, but what I also discovered was, no matter what their age, men still thought with their penises. And their penises didn't like being wrapped up in rubber. Their penises said to them, "Don't worry, fella. She's clean, and she's not going to get pregnant." Plus, at this stage of their lives, they wanted the best possible chance of getting and keeping an erection, especially those men who proudly announced, "No way; I don't need a pill to get hard."

Some of them were lying; it's a male pride thing, I suppose. Before too long, I was able to tell the difference between a chemically-induced erection and an erection 'au natural'. No, I didn't let on. Viva Viagra!

I had no rules about when I slept with someone, though typically, I didn't think it appropriate for it to happen the first time we met. After that, anything was possible.

I discovered that I was very comfortable being the initiator. I carried my "life's too short" mantra into the bedroom. Contrary to how I used to think about the wait-until-we-get-to-know-each-other-better strategic timing of sex, I now felt that it was only after I had had sex with a man I was interested in that we could get on with getting to know each other better as people. Get the first roll-in-the-hay over with, and all the anticipatory sexual tension was eliminated. Then, we could relax with each other. Plus, why would I want to invest a lot of time getting to know a man if ultimately I wasn't going to enjoy who he was in bed? Now, how's that for living in the 21st century?

Of course, there was another cautionary matter to be reckoned with: What about recent blood tests? Mine? His? Do I/does he just ask, "Have you had one recently?" And then believe the answer. Or do I/does he say, "Prove it." And oh, by the way, what's recent enough?

The whole idea of even broaching the subject seemed so foreign to me. I had heard stories of men and women who dated for a while, then decided to have sex. They went together to get blood tests. How romantic! That never happened to me.

I figured that when the time came, I'd deal with it. If a man wanted me to produce blood test results, I'd get a blood test and produce the results. But no man asked to see a blood test. Isn't that shocking? And only one man—the man who wore the condoms—even asked if I had ever gotten a blood test. I was especially shocked because all of these men knew that my husband had left me for a man. I always told them that he had not been with anyone else during our marriage, and it was true. Still, I felt, these men were taking my word for it not because they trusted me—they hardly knew me—but because that was what they wanted to believe.

Of course, even if men didn't ask me for my blood-test results, certainly I could have asked them for theirs. After all, I wasn't the only woman they had had sex with. But I didn't ask. I'm not sure why. Perhaps I put (too much?) trust in my gut instincts about the men I chose to sleep with. That, combined with the fact that I've never been a worrier. Still, I suppose, I have to consider myself lucky. I never contracted any STDs. I was never exposed to AIDS. Yes, I was lucky.

*N*ow, continue to the next chapter, or flip this book over to page 49 to see how you can do it, too.

CHAPTER SIX

Oh, The Men I Met

Oh, the stories I can tell! And I will!

Out of the 100-plus men I met over a three-year period, 15 made it beyond the meeting phase. Seven of the 15 made it to a relationship. Six made it to good friends. They still are good friends, and I'm forever grateful.

The first man I met—I'll call him Man No. 1—introduced me to a great restaurant and opened my eyes to what men lie about the most—their height. (After all, height is the number one physical trait women focus on when trolling for men.)

He was already sitting at a table and didn't get up when I arrived. It didn't bother me. (I was too liberated to expect a seated man to stand up when a woman approached.) But when dinner was over, I connected the dots. As he stood, he lifted his arms, like he was stretching. With his arms upstretched he was probably the height he had indicated in his profile! With his arms down, he was a lot shorter. Too short for me, and I'm only 5'4".

In a different It's-A-Small-World department of online dating, Man No. 2, it turned out, had worked in the same real estate office as my cousin. The first thing I did was call her to do a reality check on this guy's height. Yes, he really was 5'10". Plus, she assured me, he was good-looking and funny, too. So, I felt OK about accepting his invitation to go dancing. I knew it was risky as a first encounter, but after all, we both came with references. (He had contacted my cousin, too, about me.)

Who could have predicted that I didn't like the band and didn't like the way he danced? After an hour – a very long hour – I told him that I needed to leave. I had a Pilates class the next morning and needed to get up early, I explained. He was visibly annoyed. What was more important, he wanted to know, staying out late with him or getting up early for a Pilates class? He probably shouldn't have asked. I chose the latter. But the next morning, I woke up thinking, "Maybe my priorities were wrong." I decided to email an apology and say, "Maybe we can go out again when I don't have a Pilates class the next morning." I never heard from him.

Man No. 3 introduced me to telephone foreplay. He was such a wonderful conversationalist that we talked every night for over an hour. This went on for an entire week. I couldn't wait to meet him. When I finally did, I was totally disappointed. He wasn't anything like his phone conversations. I didn't like his looks, and he seemed to have run out of interesting things to say.

Had I – had he, too – set such high expectations based on our phone conversations that the reality could never match the fantasy? Or maybe he just wasn't my type, and I wasn't his. Still, it was a good lesson. I added, "No more protracted phone conversations" to my rule book.

Man No. 4 was so nice, so funny, so intelligent – and he professed to be instantly and totally smitten with me. He wanted to be with me all the time. I tried to sidestep it by telling him how busy I was with my work.

"I barely have time to eat dinner," I told him.

"Then I'll come to your house with food. I'll cook dinner for you. And I'm a very good cook."

No matter what I said, he made offers that should have swept me off my feet. How could I turn away such a "find"? I went out with him about five times, but it just wasn't happening for me. The chemistry wasn't there.

By the end of my first month online, I had gone out with a dozen men, and not one had lit a fire under me. What was the problem? Was it me? Was I too old? Had I been married to one man for too long? Did there have to be Chemistry? What was Chemistry, anyway? The answer came from Man No. 13.

He was a philosophy professor, and he taught me everything I needed to know about the "C" word. It started with his photograph.

He looked young for 63. (Was this an old photo?) He appeared to have a surprisingly full—it actually looked thick—head of brown (natural?) hair that he wore swept back. The combination of horn-rimmed glasses and khaki sport jacket over an olive green Izod-esque shirt gave him a preppy look. He wasn't actually smiling at the camera, but he was making excellent eye contact with it. I thought I noticed a twinkle in his eyes. I thought he looked like my father.

He described himself as an

affectionate and passionate person.

So was I!
He said that he loved

the beach, reading, music, and good food.

So did I!
He had a PhD.
So did I.
He grew up in New York City.

So had I.

He was lean/slender.

So was I.

He was very active.

So was I.

He was a left wing moderate.

Ditto.

He had turquoise eyes.

Be still my heart.

He was perfect.

During our first phone conversation we discovered an imperative to meet quickly. Each of us had travel plans that would keep us out of town for almost two weeks. We decided to meet that afternoon, if only for an hour.

It was love at first sight.

He was standing outside the restaurant when I pulled up. As strange as it sounds – and seemed – I felt, yes felt, something. Right through my car window! Was that Chemistry? The C word?

I lowered the window.

"I'm here," I said. But in my head I was saying, "You're 'The One.' I just know it. So why should we even bother with this meeting when I have so much else to do before I leave tomorrow? Let's just get together in two weeks and fuck our brains out?"

When I got out of the car and he touched my arm, I felt it again – the C word – all through my body.

I remember telling him about my summer home and how I would spend six weeks there alone because my husband could get only two weeks off from his work. He scowled and shook his head. "I never would have let my wife spend time without me."

I ignored that red flag – and all the others. There was so much about him to love. He was good-looking (we looked so cute together), intelligent, clever, funny, and creative. The sex was extraordinary. He was a great sex-ed teacher, and I surprised myself by being a motivated student. He gave me an A+.

"You're Sleeping Beauty," he told me one night when I had exceeded his expectations in bed. And mine. "I've awakened your sexuality." He was right.

But, oh, how wrong he was in other ways. All wrong.

On jdate.com, he had chosen *easygoing/flexible/open-minded* to describe himself.

But on terra firma, he was *None of Above*. Instead he was uptight, inflexible, and close-minded. He was controlling.

My heart was saying, "He's the one." My gut knew, "He's not the one."

"You know, you're really spending too much time on the phone," he would say. "I'd rather you talk on the phone when I'm not around."

But he was always around. We had started living together almost immediately. Less than a month after our first date in May, we had picked a wedding date. A year from June. And a wedding dress and shoes to match, of course, and a ring that we didn't officially call an engagement ring, but . . .

"You're moving too fast," cautioned my friends who were hearing less and less from me.

And my response was, "I want this to begin fast, so that if it's going to end, it'll end fast."

We broke up late on a Friday night, less than three months after the relationship began. Early the next morning, I went back online to start the trolling-for-men cycle again. He was already there! Viva la candy store!

Sure, I can say that now. But then, I was crushed, and it took me a long time – and a lot of men – to recover.

Yes, the world was my oyster. I was in control. I could meet someone new whenever I wanted to. And I did.

The professor, two CPAs, three architects, a handful of lawyers, two high school teachers, a Hollywood director, a used car salesman, a pilot, a minister, a former CIA agent (at least that's what he told me), a man with no body hair, and a Jewish doctor (which, momentarily, gave my Jewish Mother renewed hope in a doctor-for-a-son-in-law).

There was a Brit, a Swede, and a Dutchman. There were the poor, the rich, the very rich, and, it seemed, everything in-between. The self-employed, the underemployed, the unemployed.

Men with bladder control problems, diabetes, sexual dysfunctions, triple bypass surgery, hearing aids, canes (but no walkers).

A tennis pro, a basketball coach, heartthrobs, heart-breakers, winners, losers, and more losers.

There was a Henry, a Harry, a Larry, a Garry, a Gary, a Jay, a Ray, three Michaels, two Freds, a Ted, and a Jed. And that's just skimming the surface.

There were so many men that I started giving them nicknames: Flake Man, Coach Man, Pool Man, The Man With All The Houses, The Billionaire, Harley Boy, The Hairless Lawyer, WWD (short for World's Worst Dancer), PNC (Probable Nut Case), The Actor, The Minister (whose name changed to Psycho Man after he started stalking me), and Straight Man (whose name changed to Phone Man after we started having phone sex).

My friends encouraged me. I'd call to tell them about my latest escapade, and the first thing they wanted to know was, "What do you call him?"

Coming up with nicknames also gave me a sense of power, that feeling of being in control. Yes, there was something demeaning about it, but except for The Man With All The Houses, none of the men ever even knew their monikers. Until – perhaps – now.

Through it all, it was a fabulous ride. I even had the man I named My Fuck Buddy. Now, how many "59-year-olds" can say that?

It started with a question.

"What are you going to wear?" he asked when he called me to arrange a time and place for our first meeting. It was, I knew, an innocent question. Lots of men ask that. It's their polite way of determining if they can go casual (jeans, perhaps, which are usually very unflattering on men of a certain age). I had heard the question many times before and had always taken it at face value, but this time, I replied. "What do you want me to wear?"

I had my sexy voice on, and I have to assume that he knew it. There was a slight pause before he said, "A very short skirt and very high heels."

"I can do that," I told him. And I did.

He was waiting for me at the bar, as planned. He could see me as I walked in, and I could tell he approved. He was one of those touchy-feely types, which I typically didn't like, but this time I was game. He moved his fingers up my arm; he ran his hand up my leg toward my thigh. Then, he paused.

"No stockings?"

"You like stockings, even with high heeled sandals?" I asked.

"Mmm, yes," he said. (That confirmed it for me. Men don't understand the finer points of fashion; they just want slutty.)

I found him terribly boring, but very sexy. When he asked whether I'd like to get together again, I said yes. We picked two nights later to get together for dinner. That morning, he called me to confirm and to let me in on a secret, a Victoria's Secret.

"I bought something for you," he told me.

"What is it?"

"Stockings from Victoria's Secret."

"The kind that need garter belts?"

"No, the kind that stay up by themselves."

I had an idea.

"Bring them to the restaurant with you. I'll take them into the ladies room and put them on."

He liked that idea. (I knew he would.)

I liked his choice of stockings. Skin-toned and very silky. They fit me perfectly. Not only my legs, but also my mindset.

Luckily, we sat at a booth with an ample tablecloth covering the exposed end of the table. No one could see him stroking my silky leg that I had placed between his legs. My shoe off, I pressed my toes against what was clearly his hard-on.

But he was still terribly boring.

"Your place or mine?" I asked him after turning down the server's dessert and/or coffee query and indicating that we were ready for the check.

He chose mine.

He had a toned body and a good erection. The sex was good, very good for a first time. When it was over, he wanted to talk. I wanted him to leave.

Note to self: "From now on, go to his place." Then, when it's over, I can leave quickly.

I agreed to see him again. "How about dinner and maybe we can go to a movie after?" he asked me.

"That sounds great." I replied. It was a lie. I had decided that for me this relationship could only be about sex.

When I called to tell him that "unfortunately" I was way too busy for dinner and the movie, I added, "I think you might just have to be My Fuck Buddy," laughing coyly and trying to make it seem as though it was a new idea, one that had just popped into my head.

I liked the arrangement. An hour or so out of an evening for some good, sometimes very good, sex worked just fine for me. I liked the feeling of control. It was totally on my terms, and I felt very empowered.

One night, as I was leaving his condo, I stopped in front of the mirror in his entryway. For some inexplicable reason, I took my lipstick out of my purse and started applying it to my lips.

"This is probably what call girls do on their way to their next trick," I thought to myself. To My Fuck Buddy, who was watching me, I said, "I feel like a prostitute."

"You're not a prostitute." he replied, sounding very caring.

"No, you don't understand," I told him. "I think I like the idea." And then, laughing, "Give me some money."

"Oh no, I couldn't," he said. He seemed appalled by my request.

"Just give me a dollar."

"No, I couldn't."

"Please," I begged. "I'll give it back to you."

"No," he said.

In an inexplicable way, I felt letdown. The fun was gone; the party was over.

He was a nice guy and always insisted on walking me to my car, kissing me good-night. This night was no different.

And just like all the other nights, I told him, "I'll call you." But this time it was a lie. Being in control felt good, but I needed more than My Fuck Buddy.

At age 55, Flake Man was the youngest man I dated. He got his nickname because he was, well, flaky. We had made plans to get together via email. He sent me his cell phone number and gave me directions to his house. The directions were wrong, and when I tried calling him, I discovered he had given me the wrong phone number. When I finally arrived, he was asleep under a tree in his front yard.

I had been very attracted to his profile and overlooked – at least for the moment – his desired age range of 47 to 53. His PhD was in education (so was mine), and he even wrote about some of the educational tenets that he strongly believed in – the same that I strongly believed in. He said that he was happy with his life — a glass-half-full statement that made me smile. Like so many other men, he said that he liked to take walks on the beach, but this time I believed it. His house was within walking distance of a beach I was familiar with. Still, I hesitated because of the age thing. And then I decided to write the following:

I'm too old for you — not even 59 as my profile says; I'm 62 — but could we just take a walk on the beach one morning and talk about education?

After, when I told my friends about it, they insisted that it was a clever ploy, a totally disingenuous come-on. But I swear, I was thinking out of the box; I meant every word of it.

As it turned out, we had a wonderful walk along the beach, talking about education — and more. When I bought up the subject of his Desired Age Range, he said, "It was there. I had to fill it in with some numbers." His response confirmed what I had been thinking all along. Most men will make exceptions in the age department because it's "just a number" they have to fill in. Not all of them, of course, especially when they first join the site. Sometimes it takes them awhile to discover that the age range they desire doesn't necessarily desire them.

Flake Man and I dated for almost six months, the longest relationship I had had.

He was the man who wouldn't have sex with me until he felt we knew each other "really well."

"I've never done it that way before," I had told him, "but I'll give it a try."

It was a four-month wait, and I never understood what made him think he knew me "really well" at that point. When we finally had sex, it was awful, and nothing seemed to be quite the same after that. He told me that I wasn't the same person he had known before. I told him that I didn't want to see him anymore. The problem was, we had already planned a three-week trip to South Africa. I was ready to cancel. He said that we should go — "as friends, the friends we were before we had sex," he told me. Acquiescing was a big mistake. The day we arrived, he wanted to have sex. No way. How could he be so deceitful? It made me so angry that a week into the trip, I changed my plane reservations, went home – and left him in South Africa

I didn't meet men only in my home states of Massachusetts and Florida. I met men on my travels, too. Vancouver, Canada; Nashville, Tennessee; New York City. When I was feeling desperate in Massachusetts, I'd expand my geographic parameters and contact men from New Hampshire, Vermont, and Maine, but nothing ever materialized. Once, when I was feeling desperate in South Florida, I started dating a man in Orlando. I actually liked the distance between us.

A 67-year-old man from California who wrote in his profile that he could "relocate for the real thing," initiated contact with me. I was intrigued. I liked his profile. He wrote:

I'm well-read, romantic, affectionate, open, honest, aware and full of fun – sometimes silly, sometimes wily . . .

He asked for my phone number. I gave it to him. I liked our ensuing lengthy phone conversation. We talked about "meeting halfway" and posed a couple of weekend destination possibilities. We were both going to check airfares, and, he said, he'd get back to me. He never did.

But it was fun to anticipate, to fantasize. More fun to think, "How great if this happens" than "It'll never happen." It was a mindset that got me through the false starts, the dashed hopes.

It's strange how things do happen.

It was a week before I'd be celebrating my third anniversary of online dating. Celebrating was probably not the right word. Let's just say, I would be observing the anniversary of three years of online dating. And what did I have to show for it? I was seeing a man who was all wrong for me. I called him Harley (as in Harley Davidson) Boy, not because he had one, but because he wanted one.

His profile had me hooked:

Creative, adventurous, exploring and family values are some of my strongest qualities. I'm ready for a committed relationship, sharing our time and activities while maintaining our individuality. The woman I want by my side is emotionally available, true to her heart, adventurous, inquisitive, sexy, family oriented, keeps a smile on her face and a song in her heart that holds her apart from the rest. It's of little concern to me what she eats, where she worships or how well her portfolio looks. My desire to be with her is paramount to all the things that we could and would do together.

I found his sense of humor, and his sensibility, seductive. Under "For Fun," he wrote:

One of my favorite things is to discover a lady slipper in the pines. One of my least favorite events is to suddenly discover a renegade shell in my soft boiled egg.

Under "Favorite Things":

Green is a favorite color, but yellow could be my mood for a day (bright, not mellow). When it rains outside, I grab a slicker.

Under "My Religion":

I've been baptized 3 times, that's how I learned how to swim. If I have to do it again, I'll bring a life jacket.

I had been mesmerized by his photo. There was a twinkle in his eyes that absolutely captivated me, and I told him so in my first email to him.

I should have called him Wrong Man. But once again (think: philosophy professor), it was all about the chemistry – from the moment we met. It was that palpable feeling, permeating my body, all over again.

He said he felt it, too, but that didn't make him any more available. He was elusive about committing to dates, and even when he did commit, he rarely kept his commitment. There were the last-minute excuses, elicited only after my frequent phone calls and emails. I had become a different person – someone I didn't want to be.

"What's better?" I asked myself. "To have my heart broken by someone I care about or to go out with men I couldn't care less about?" Faulty thinking?

When am I going to fall in love with someone who's right for me? Wishful thinking?

What made matters worse, as anniversary No. 3 approached, was the harsh reality that I would be turning 63 in less than two months, and I refused to break the two rules I had lived by for three years.

1) I would not lie about my age by more than three years. I had been 57, 58, 59 for the past three years. I would have to go to the big Six-O now. I couldn't stand the thought of it.

2) I would not keep photos posted that were more than two years old. I was just about to cross that threshold. I couldn't stand the thought of it.

I felt as though I was coming to the end of my rope. I had already given up on ever finding Mr. Right. Now, it looked like I would have to give up on finding My Travel Buddy. And I would go off online dating entirely. But really, I had no regrets. I reminded myself I had worked the system in all the ways that worked for me. I hadn't sat around waiting for Prince Charmings to knock on my door; I had gone knocking on theirs. I wasn't so picky that I limited my prospects, and as a result, I had met so many interesting people who had, in one way or another, enhanced my life. I had reinvented myself numerous times, and I was a better person for it.

Sure, I wished I had found someone who liked me as much as I liked him, maybe even loved me, but still, it felt good to know that, over the three years, more men liked me than I liked them. It had taken decades, but I was no longer the teenager with no dates. What fun to be popular, at any age!

No, I had absolutely no regrets. I would be fine. My three-year run was up, and I was ready to acknowledge what I could take away from the experience – six wonderful male friends who were always there for me. And what about Harley Boy? One of these days, it will end, I told myself, and sooner or later I'd get over him.

But first, I would spend one last week – my third anniversary week – on Match.com trolling for men.

By now, the search wasn't taking nearly as long as it once had – even at its slowest periods. The returns had been diminishing for a while. Gone were the days when I could come up with 50 out of 500 men I wanted to meet. This time I came up with only 10; but one of them seemed absolutely fabulous. I liked his looks and loved his profile (right down to every perfectly placed comma and semi-colon). He came across as intelligent, introspective, caring, and witty. OK, so he liked children and dogs. I'd deal with it.

He wrote:

I would match best with a woman who shares some of my interests, but is open to new adventures as I am. I like children (three of my own, grown) and big good-natured dogs, but please don't go out and get any on my account. I prefer bright attractive women with a sense of humor and style, passionate about the important things in their life, but able to leave their competitiveness behind them when we're together. Most of all I like to spend time with someone who likes to spend time with me.

Under the heading "My Education," he wrote:

The older you get, the more you realize what you learn about is people, especially yourself.

Under the heading "Favorite Things," he wrote:

Love fireplaces, not gas logs; love French White Burgundy, not oakie Chardonnays; love outdoor sports, not gym workouts; love Monopoly, not Parcheesi.

See what I mean? Wasn't he great? I held my breath, hoping that he would respond to my "Wow" email. And he did:

Thanks for contacting me, and for the compliment. I have recently been overwhelmed by the combination of working and my coaching. Certainly your profile looks interesting. I hope you don't mind if I contact you a little later.

Well, that was definitely the nicest brush-off I had received in three years.

Yes, I wrote right back. I told him I'd be happy to wait and controlled myself from asking for his definition of "a little later." I still haven't heard from him.

Another wrote back:

Thank you for your complimentary email. You are a very attractive and fun-sounding person, but I think I am a bit too old for you. In addition, my situation with an 18-year-old boy entering college along with general financial concerns is going to limit my lifestyle in the future. I wish you all the best.

No, I didn't bother to write back to tell him my real age.

Another responded:

You are very kind to write. I enjoyed your profile and your honesty, but this probably is not the right match at this time for me.

I sent an email to the man who had described himself as:

a financially secure, responsible man in search of an attractive and intelligent woman with similar interests such as traveling and good food.

Did he say, travel?

And he wrote back:

Hi Dale: The big question is, why are we here now? It is still freezing, and we may get more snow tomorrow. Would you like to get together for coffee, a cocktail, or even lunch? My schedule is pretty flexible seeing that I'm retired. I look forward to your reply.

Now, that could be promising, I thought, even though my gut was saying, "It doesn't sound as though he has a life." I sent him my phone number, and he called. My gut was right. His schedule sounded just a tad too flexible for me. He sounded just a tad too boring. I decided not to see him.

The week wasn't up yet. I went back to the virtual drawing board and, in desperation, expanded my geographic sights and wrote to someone in Portland, Maine. I was struck by the fact that he and I had the same tag lines, and pointed that out to him in my "Wow" email. Alas, he wasn't interested in a long-distance relationship, but his response almost made me relocate to Portland. It also confirmed how important photos are. In response to my email, he wrote:

Thank you for your kind words and enthusiasm for my profile. Yes, I think it was our phrase 'Come Fly With Me' that caught my eye, but your picture also jolted me out of that robotic state one lapses into occasionally while running through the gauntlet of Match profiles.

I do have a hard-won aversion to long-distance liaisons just because they seem to impart a certain artificiality to each personal encounter.

To tell you the truth, I was a little intimidated by how beautiful I thought you were. You would be just about my ideal find from the standpoint of physical appearance (only one parameter in the total mix of things to be sure). That black dress and how you cocked your right heel up off the floor just about sent me into a coma—the others nearly finished me off. I thought: this woman must

*have guys falling all over her, oozing out of her mailbox, and clogging up her
washer-dryer vent.*

Now do you see why I almost moved to Portland?

That week, as in the past, I received a handful of emails from
men who initiated contact with me. And, as usual, they weren't
anyone I was interested in.

One man wrote:

*You are a very beautiful woman, and I like your profile. I am a very loving
and affectionate man and I'm looking for the same in a woman. I'm also looking for a long term relationship. If your curious or interested, please write.*

Clearly, this was a man who had not read my profile. He just
looked at my photos, then sent his form letter. I was neither curious nor interested, and thought, "This is exactly why I'm ready to
spend the rest of my social life with my six male friends."

And then, on April 17, one day after my third anniversary
online, another unsolicited man wrote:

Hello, my name is Thom. Want to chat a little and see what happens?

Why in the world had he written to me? More important, why
in the world did I respond?

Before I attempt to answer that question (not that there actually is an answer), I need to say something about how sending an
email works on Match.com.

First, I write an email to someone. Then I hit "send." The next
page that appears is a message from Match:

"If you like _____ (the online name of person you just wrote
to appears here), check out these members."

I had decided that there was an underlying message here. Why
be satisfied with the person you just wrote to when there are all
these other people out there? The candy store mentality.

But wait. There was more. If you were satisfied with the person you just wrote to, you'd end up canceling your membership,

and, I figured, that's the last thing online dating services want to see happen—no matter what they say to the contrary. If they really found everyone a match, they'd be out of business!

And what made me scratch my head, then laugh out loud, was that the profiles that appeared were very rarely people who had any similarity to the person I had just written to.

And the men usually didn't even fall within my age criteria—and vice versa. Many of them lived clear across the country!

But I couldn't help looking. Just for kicks. I don't think I had ever found anyone of interest on that "check out these (other) members" page. But this time it was different. Looking right at me was a very nice-looking 66-year-old who lived only 10 miles away. And he was smiling at me with a very intriguing, open-my-profile-now smile.

I read his tagline:

There are a few things I haven't done for so long I may have forgotten how. I may need a coach.

Hmm. Now, what could that mean? I thought I knew exactly what it meant. He hadn't had sex, and he was worried that he wouldn't be able to perform. But hadn't I always been turned off by profiles with sexual innuendoes? Why was I thinking now that a man who was able to put that out there appealed to me? Why did I find it titillating? Why was I suddenly thinking that this could be a very interesting, uh, challenge?

And why, as I read his profile, did I overlook all the other deal breakers?

Not only did he have a son, but his son sometimes lived at home. And, to make matters worse, he had posted a photo of himself with his son. And a photo of himself with a boat. And a photo of himself with a fishing pole. Later, when I looked more closely at his primary photo—the one that made me open his profile—I noticed that the background was a golf course, and he was wearing a cap. How many of my deal breakers was that!

He wrote in the "For Fun" category:

In the summer, I'm on the golf course a lot, but I also like to hike in the mountains, fly fish, sail and sometimes sit in the shade with a good book. Fall is hunting season and I have annual trips for birds and ducks. Winter is for skiing.

He wrote in the "Favorite Hot Spots" section:

I like to travel with an activity as its purpose such as sailing, trekking, shooting, golf, whatever.

He listed himself as a political conservative, and under smoking habits, he put down "No answer." What if that meant he smoked cigarettes? What would I do then? Fortunately, my Scarlett O'Hara kicked in. "I'll think about that tomorrow," I told myself.

Even now as I write this, I wonder, how was I attracted to a man with a son who sometimes lives at home; a man who plays golf; a man who hikes, sails, skis, and shoots? Shoots! Hadn't I written a profile (the one I never posted) that said men who play golf or hike or ski or kayak (isn't that another word for sailing?) need not apply? I had never responded to a man who listed himself as politically conservative. I had refused to write to men who were "newbies" – men who had been online for less than four, even six, months. As far as I was concerned, newbies were too full of themselves because of all the women who were contacting them. Instant popularity went straight to their heads. Give them four to six months, and they'll come back down to earth, or they'll be in a relationship, was my way of thinking.

Why in the world wasn't I hitting Next?

Maybe it was our similarities, similarities about the bigger things. Like our outlook on life. It sounded like he really saw the glass half full, that he lived life to its fullest, that he took risks, that he was spontaneous and even-tempered. And not only was he involved in a career, but he also sounded as though he loved what he was doing, and what he was doing was real estate. He wrote:

I've been involved with commercial real estate most of my working life and plan to do it as long as I can.

Here was someone who, like me, loved real estate and never wanted to retire, someone who could obviously travel without compromise. And he wanted a woman who was

Attractive, outgoing, independent and is willing to take some initiative.

That's me!

I don't think I had ever read a man's profile that included the word "initiative." I loved taking initiative. The idea of a man actually wanting that made me feel lightheaded, especially a man who sounded like he took his own initiative, too.

And what about a "relationship"?

He wrote:

I'm not looking for a serious relationship, but I'm not opposed to it either.

Well now, wasn't that pretty much the essence of my profile when I wrote:

Need I say, this is not your garden-variety relationship? It's not about 'one-and-only.' (I've already had mine.) Or holding hands on the beach (though I don't rule that out).

I beefed up my standard *"Wow"* email, by adding:

Real estate, travel, and movies. Oh, my.

I wanted him to respond so badly, I could taste it. And, in less than 24 hours, he did. He wrote:

Wow back. I must say your profile is one of the best I've read. Your description of what you like and what you want instead of statements about things someone else will be the judge of is very refreshing. I think you are looking for me! But I guess you will be the judge of that. I just returned from South Carolina and have yet to unpack. Before we book flights, maybe we ought to meet?

He had put his phone number below his name (Peter), and I called him as soon as I calmed down from reading his wonderfully upbeat, insightful, and funny email. I had never believed in waiting. (Don't look too eager? Oh, who cares?)

It was a surprisingly short conversation. But long enough to ask him my requisite questions: "How long have you been on Match? (Answer: three months.) How has it been so far? (Answer: Met twelve women; seeing four of them – casually.)

The conversation was long enough for me to figure it all out. He could be my distraction, a way to take my mind off Harley Boy, the man-who-was-totally-wrong-for-me. Well, not exactly take my mind off Harley Boy; just give me a chance to think about something (someone?) else every once in a while. After all, Peter wouldn't possibly have enough available time – not with his four other casual relationships – to interfere with my seeing Harley Boy whenever Harley Boy wanted to see me.

Yes, this would definitely work. The timing couldn't be better for – what should I call it/him? – a Fuck 'N' Travel Buddy. Now, there's a perfect combination. Add him to my six male friends, and I might just have Composite Man. Ever since I had come to the conclusion that I would never find one man to satisfy all my needs, I had come up with the idea of Composite Man – a group of men actually who, combined, would satisfy all my needs.

Yes, this would work perfectly. The glass is half full.

And then, we met.

*N*ow, continue to the next chapter, or flip this book over to page 55 to see how you can do it, too.

CHAPTER SEVEN

And She Lived Happily Ever After

He knew the restaurant I suggested, one that I had met many men at in the past. We planned on meeting there at 6 p.m. because Gary—my New York friend who had helped me with the profile that attracted Peter to me—was driving up for the weekend. When I walked into the restaurant, the hostess asked me if I was meeting someone named Peter.

"He just called to let you know that he'd be about 10 minutes late."

What an impression that made on me! A man who would actually call the restaurant to tell me that he was going to be late by 10 minutes. That was a first.

"Would you like to sit down at the table and wait?" she asked me.

I couldn't. I was too jumpy. So I went back to my car. I wanted to call Peter to say that I had gotten his message, and to tell him that I had parked in front of the restaurant and I was saving the space in front of me for him. Peter pulled up. I looked in my rearview mirror to check how I looked for one last time and said (out loud), "Here comes my distraction."

We spent three-and-a-half hours in that restaurant. Asking, answering, talking, listening, laughing; asking, answering, talking, listening, laughing.

He admitted to enjoying sitting in front of his computer and searching through women's profiles. He liked to look at their photos and, if the photos sparked his curiosity, he would read their profiles. But he never contacted any of them. He didn't have to. He was too busy as it was responding to the emails women were sending him. He couldn't believe what was happening to him. His head was spinning.

So many women, so little time.

He was obviously a gentleman – operating by the dating rules he remembered from the late '60s and early '70s. When he took out a woman for the first time, he would ask her out for a second date, whether or not he really wanted to. (They all accepted.) He did it because he thought that was the right thing to do. He hadn't yet been indoctrinated into The New Dating Game.

Of course, I wondered, why in the world does a man like this 'need' to be doing online dating? I asked; he answered.

"As soon as everyone knew that my marriage had ended," he told me, "all the married women were trying to fix me up with their single friends, but I wouldn't do that. If I went out with someone's friend, and I didn't like her, I'd be disappointing two people."

There was more.

"I'd be dating in a fishbowl. If my next door neighbor fixed me up, there'd be some explaining to do when I didn't take the woman out the second time; and everyone at the Club would know about it."

It was clear to me that I wanted to be part of this man's life. Even if I had to be one of five.

"Just as long as I'm No. 1 of five," I told myself. To get there fast, I needed to think fast.

"Are you having sex with any of the four women you're seeing?" (Yes, I really asked him that.)

"No."

"Why not?" (Yes, I really asked him that, too.)

"At this point, I just want to keep the relationships casual. It's been so long. I don't know what I'm really looking for. If I were to have sex with any of them, it would put the relationship into a different category."

"And you're scared, too." (I was testing out whether my initial take on his profile was correct.)

"Yes. I haven't had sex in seven years." (Bingo!)

"Don't worry." I told him. Then, I paused. Maybe it was for the dramatic effect. Or maybe it was to think about what I was about to say once more before I said it. "I'll be your Fuck Buddy."

How did he respond? This is the part I can't remember, though I do know that he had a positive reaction. (Weeks later, he would tell me that he also had a hard-on, caused by my unexpected offer.)

I continued: "You can be my distraction which I definitely need."

I didn't go into great detail about Harley Boy. Just enough to let it be known that maybe I wasn't seeing four other people, but I was seeing one other person. And it had been going on for a while. (Read: I'm not a total loser.)

Later that night, I re-thought my offer.

"You know," I told him. "I misspoke. I don't want us to be Fuck Buddies; I want us to be Friends With Benefits."

I explained the distinction.

A Friend With Benefits was somewhere between Fuck Buddy and serious relationship. It wasn't just about sex, but it wasn't about getting emotionally entwined. We'd have sex – and we'd do other things, but in a casual, noncommittal way. As friends.

When it was time to leave, he said that he'd like to see me again and wondered whether we could get together on Sunday afternoon after Gary left. "We could go to dinner and a movie," he told me.

"What, no sex?" I thought, laughing to myself at my little joke.

We stood at his car, and he kissed me. It was a long kiss, and I remember it. He remembers more:

"I kissed you and you looked at me, and you said, 'We're going to have fun.'"

The fun part made a big impression on him. It was what he was looking for; I was offering it to him.

Gary listened as I described the three-plus hours I had just spent with Peter.

"What do you call him?" he asked me.

"Peter," I replied.

"He doesn't have a nickname?" He was incredulous. I could see it in his eyes.

"No. But if he did, it would be 'Perfect Man'."

Perfect Man?

(That was the voice in my head talking.) How could that be? He has a son who sometimes lives at home (deal breaker); his political leanings are totally askew (deal breaker); he shoots guns (it was never on my deal breaker list because I never imagined a man even admitting to that; dare I even ask if he's a member of the NRA?); he kayaks, skis, hikes (deal breakers); he plays golf. (You gotta be kidding!)

Perfect Man. His smile, his laugh, the way he looked at me when he spoke; his obvious honesty; the questions he asked; his values; his ethics; his belief system; his personality that no one can describe in words in a profile no matter how hard one tries.

I was a wreck the entire weekend, though I tried not to show it to Gary. After all, he was a house guest, not a therapist. Those damn insecurities had reared their ugly heads once again.

Is Peter really going to see me Sunday, or was he just being polite? After all, he had said, "I'll call you Sunday afternoon." Not "Call me when your friend leaves."

Did I wait for him to call me? Of course not. As soon as Gary left I called Peter.

"That's it," my insecurities told me. "He's there; he sees the caller ID. He's not going to pick up. He has no intention of seeing you."

Of course, my insecurities were wrong. He called (when he got back from the golf course and listened to my message).

"Come over, and we'll look in the paper and see what movie is playing that we both want to see," he suggested.

On the way, my car broke down.

"Are you lost?" he asked me when I called to tell him what happened.

"I wish," I replied. I told him where I was (at a gas station waiting to be towed to a repair shop), and he came to rescue this damsel in distress. Strange that right from the beginning, I wasn't the tough, independent broad I had been putting out there whenever I met/dated/slept with a man. I even let him do some of the talking when we got to the repair shop.

"What's going on here?" that voice in my head asked. "You're letting a man–this man–negotiate for you?" But somehow I didn't think that Peter was doing it because he didn't think I could. He was doing it because he was a nice guy. A gentleman. Still, the voice repeated itself:

"What's going on here?"

We moved to his car. He held the door open for me. He took me to his house. I got out of the car before he could open the door for me. We looked in the paper to see if there was a movie we both wanted to see, and there wasn't. The movie I had wanted to see he had already seen – with one of the four other women.

"We'll watch a DVD," he said, "but let's go to dinner first."

He chose a nearby Chinese restaurant where the food was good and, I thought, the service was quick. Back at his house, we decided to watch *The Big Chill*. What a perfect choice! We had both seen it so many times before that we didn't really need to watch it to know what was going on; and anyway, what was going on between the two of us on the couch was much more exciting.

"Let's go upstairs," he said, as he hit the pause button. He led me up the staircase and into his bedroom.

I knew I could do it; I knew he could do it. I was the coach he had been looking for in his profile, but none of the other four women had been smart enough to volunteer for the job.

How can I put into words what happened? When he climaxed, I felt as though we connected not just sexually, but emotionally. He felt it, too.

When it was over, I got out of bed and went into the bathroom. When I came out, he was standing there, holding a bathrobe – his bathrobe – for me, the arms outstretched. He had a big smile on his face. I walked toward the bathrobe slowly, then turned around so that I could put my arms through the sleeves. Still standing behind me, he wrapped the body of the robe around me, tied the belt, and held me there, close.

He's opening up his life to me, I thought, and I've just entered it.

We walked back down the stairs, and I realized that everything felt totally different. We had walked up the stairs as strangers. When we walked down the stairs, there was a bond between us that we never could have imagined. This time we weren't two people on the couch; we were one. I nestled in his lap, and we finished watching *The Big Chill*. Then, as two avid Red Sox fans, we watched our team play one of the most exciting games of the season. How fitting!

Then, we went back upstairs, and I took off the robe.

The next day he drove me into Boston; he went to his office while I met a friend for lunch.

"What do you call him?" she asked me.

"Peter," I said.

He met me outside his office, and he was smiling.

"Why are you smiling?" I asked.

"Because I'm so happy," he replied.

My car was ready. He drove me to the repair shop. As we got closer, we started talking about our upcoming availability. He was booked solid for the week. I was supposed to see Harley Boy on Thursday.

"What's wrong with me?" I wondered. "As right as I'm feeling about Peter, I'm still looking forward to a date with the man who's all wrong for me?"

On Saturday, I was leaving for New York; from there I was going to Nashville and ending up in Fort Lauderdale where I would be staying until the following Tuesday. I simply couldn't stand the thought of 10 days without Peter. But wasn't it too soon to let him know that? How would I feel if he rejected my proposal? I knew I had to take the risk.

"Do you want to spend next weekend in Florida with me?" I blurted out, as we pulled up to the repair shop.

And he said, "Yes." Without even hesitating.

The weekend together turned into six days together. Glorious days. Incredible nights. On the way to the airport, he told me, "I need to call the four other women and let them know that I can't see them anymore."

"Are you sure it's not too soon?" I asked, not because I wanted to, but because I thought I should.

"No," he said.

And over the next two days, he called (not emailed) them. He said he didn't want me to be around when he did it, so I stayed at my house. When he had made the four phone calls, he invited me back to his house, and I never left.

He likes to say, "Our first date lasted three-and-a-half hours; our second date lasted 24 hours; our third date lasted . . . We're still on our third date."

My friends admit that they greeted the news that I had met the man of my dreams with great joy, but a little disappointment, too. My stories wouldn't be as interesting as they had been before. Even my manicurist noted that she had looked forward to, and now missed, my weekly date updates.

For my male friends still floundering on Match.com, I suddenly became the "poster child." They started analyzing what it was that I had done over the previous three years to make this happen. They all came to the same conclusion, articulated by one of them: "I don't know anyone who's worked as hard on this as you have."

Yes, I definitely worked hard. It would have been easy to compromise, but I didn't. It would have been easy to disregard my first impressions of a man, but I didn't. It would have been easy to see the glass half empty, but I worked at always seeing it half full.

Even at its worst, I'd walk away from meeting someone awful, forcing myself to find something I had gained from the experience. Even if it was a cup of coffee with a different flavor shot.

It would have been extremely easy to not keep going, but I kept going. Even when I decided to stop looking for the "right" man, it was because I felt I had reached a goal—a different goal—that I had set for myself. I found and used survival techniques that worked for me, and when they stopped working, I found and used others.

I used online dating to my advantage, and I used men to my advantage (which is not a bad thing). I grew from every experience because I learned something about myself from every man I met. I reinvented myself several times over. Not for someone else, but for myself. And I kissed enough frogs to get to my prince. I was right. It's a matter of numbers. I didn't know what my number was. It ended up being somewhere between 100 and 125. And it took me three years to get there. Peter didn't know his number either. His was 13, and it took him less than three months. Yes, everyone has a number.

I have never been loved so much, nor have I loved so much. I have myself to thank.

*I*f you've been going from one chapter on this side to one chapter on the other side, flip this book over to page 65 to see how you can do it, too.

*I*f you've been reading this entire side of the book, flip this book over to page 1 to see how you can do it, too.

THE

and

INTELLIGENT

you'll

WOMAN'S

live

GUIDE TO

happily

ONLINE

ever after

DATING

By Dale Koppel, PhD.

Online dating is the journey.

Use it as a roadmap to reach your destination.

CONTENTS

How To Read This Book   ix

Preface   xiii

Acknowledgments   xvii

CHAPTER ONE:

   INTRODUCTION: HOW I DID IT   1

CHAPTER TWO:

   FIRST, THE PHOTOS: HOW I DID IT   7

CHAPTER THREE:

   NEXT, THE PROFILE: HOW I DID IT   11

CHAPTER FOUR:

   TROLLING FOR MEN: HOW I DID IT

   Step 1: The Search   27

   Step 2: The Initial Contact   40

   Step 3: Hopefully, The Response   41

   Step 4: The Meeting   43

CHAPTER FIVE:

    WHAT ABOUT SEX: HOW I DID IT   61

CHAPTER SIX:

    OH, THE MEN I MET   69

CHAPTER SEVEN:

    AND SHE LIVED HAPPILY EVER AFTER   93

BOOK TWO:
HOW YOU CAN DO IT TOO

CHAPTER ONE

Introduction:
You Can Do It Too

Once upon a time, there was no online dating. You had to hope that you'd meet a man at a bar or a party or in the produce section of your local supermarket. Maybe a friend would fix you up. And if you were lucky, the guy would be halfway decent. But that was a rarity.

When online dating first started in the mid-1990s, a lot of people were ashamed to admit they had signed up. There was a stigma attached, a stigma that online dating was a last resort. An embarrassment. It said, "I'm a loser. I can't meet a man any other way. Now I have to resort to this."

Not true. Where else can you spend a couple of hours "meeting" hundreds of men? Men who meet specific criteria that you select. Age, geographic location, educational background, political leaning.

Anyone who's looking for a man and isn't online is absolutely crazy. And anyone who's online and won't admit it is crazy, too. Tell someone that you're on an online dating site and inevitably their

1

response will be a variation on a theme: "Oh, my best friend's sister-in-law did online dating, and that's how she met her husband." How reinforcing is that? Trust me, you could be at your most demoralized, and when you hear those words, you'll perk up. "There's (still) hope for me," you'll say to yourself. And you're right.

It's not just about finding an online dating service. It's about finding the best online dating service for you, and only you can determine that by taking the time to visit the sites and checking out profiles. Which one seems to have members who are most appealing to you? Do you want to join a special interest site with fewer members or one with the largest and broadest membership base? You don't have to join more than one (save your money for a great pair of shoes)–unless you really want to. And you shouldn't join for less than three months when you first get started. That's because you want to give it a chance (none of this 30-day "trial" period, please) and really soak your feet in it. It's not about trying it out to see if it fits; it's about trying it on to see how it fits. You shouldn't re-join for more than six months. That's because you always want to have a sense of flexibility.

Once you've picked the best site (for you), the real work begins. Posting your best photos, writing your best profile, and actively working the system. When you do, you'll meet men. Lots of them.

The more men you meet, the better your chance of meeting the special one–or special ones. The more frogs you kiss, the closer you'll get to the prince. It's a numbers game, after all. We all hope for a low number, but it doesn't always work that way. And unfortunately, we never know what our number is. Until we reach it.

So, be prepared to work hard. Put yourself out there. The biggest mistake you can make is to wait for men to come to you. If there's one word you need to repeat to yourself, it's the "P" word: Proactive. Putting yourself out there isn't just about posting photos and a profile, then sitting there and waiting for the men to contact you. No, it's about you contacting men, men, and more men. This

is a job, but the good news is, you're your own boss. You make your own hours, and a lot of it is going to be in the privacy of your own home, searching the site for men who look interesting enough to contact. Hey, you can do it in your underwear!

But even before you take your clothes off, there's a lot of cerebral preparation. A lot of thinking, questioning, soul-searching. It's not just about choosing the site, then writing your profile. It's about taking a good, hard look at yourself and deciding whether there are any major decisions you have to make about yourself. I'm talking about your personality, your appearance, your outlook, your goals. You're the one who has to decide whether there are things you truly don't like about yourself. I'm talking about plastic surgery, dental work, an exercise regimen, weight loss, weight gain (yes, you could be too thin), therapy, life coaching, anti-depressants, electrolysis, quitting smoking. But only if you – and only you – think it's necessary.

If you think it's necessary, get it done before you join an online dating service. There's nothing wrong with saying, "This is my one-year plan. At the end of the year, when I've accomplished my personal goals, that's when I'll be ready to join an online dating site."

Then, there's the whole notion of emotional readiness – a divorce, a death, the demise of a lengthy relationship.

I'm a believer in sooner rather than later for the following reasons: It's going to be difficult no matter how long it takes. You're going to go through the same trials and tribulations no matter how long it takes. You are going to have to follow the same rules to succeed no matter how long it takes. Life's short. Do it now.

Still, no one but you can determine how long a mourning period you need.

OK, so you're ready. You still need to prepare yourself emotionally for what's in store, especially the inevitable rejections. (Remember, if you never allow yourself to be rejected, you'll never have the opportunity to be accepted.)

In the worst of times, come up with mantras, like "This too shall pass" or "There are hundreds more where he came from." Both are absolutely true. Sure, it's going to feel demoralizing in a what's-wrong-with-me sort of way. And you may actually need to look at what's wrong with you, and then make the necessary changes. That doesn't mean changing who you are (unless you really want to); it means changing expectations, setting new goals, creating new realities.

Always remember – and keep reminding yourself – that you're in charge here. No, I'm not kidding. You really are in control. It's all about how you see it, how you work the system. Make your own rules, and play by those rules. But never get locked into them. Give them a chance, but if they stop working for you, feel free to change them just as you should feel free to change your photos, your profile, your online dating site.

Don't be surprised if your expectations and goals are too lofty in the beginning. There's nothing wrong with modifying them; that's the way you stay in control. That's the way you ameliorate disappointment. In the beginning, it's hard not to expect that the man you're meeting tonight is going to be "The One." After a while, your expectation will be: "The man I meet tonight will enrich my life in some way." At other times it will be: "Well, it's better than watching TV alone" (though sometimes it's not). At all times it will be: "Here's a new story to tell my friends."

So, welcome to the wacky world of online dating. It's a veritable roller coaster ride. The highs, the lows, the lowers. One step forward, two steps back. At least that's how it'll often feel. But there'll be many times that you will be taking steps forward and none back.

You've heard it before, I'm sure: Set realistic expectations, and you won't be disappointed.

Just don't mistake "realistic" for low." Set low expectations, and you'll live down to them. Does that mean you've reached your goal? Answer: Not if your low expectations aren't what you really want.

It doesn't matter how old you are. Age is only a number, especially when you make online dating work for you. I did. You can, too. I felt in control. You can, too.

You'll laugh; you'll cry. Your heart will be broken; you'll break a heart or two. You'll learn something, you'll grow from every experience you have, even the worst of them. I did. You will, too.

*N*ow, continue to the next chapter, or flip this book over to page 7 to see how how *I* did it.

CHAPTER TWO

First, The Photos:
How To Do it

I cannot say this enough: Men are all about the photos. It hardly matters what you say in your profile. If you're a knockout, you could describe yourself as an axe murderer, and you'll still hear from men. That's because they'll take one look at your photos and not even bother reading what you've written. Well, maybe I'm exaggerating, but not by much.

Men have told me that the first thing they read is how a woman describes her body type–especially when she only posts a head shot. The men who've been around the online dating block a few times become very jaded. They morph into non-believers.

Every online dating service asks its members to describe their body type. Way too many women choose average, even when, in a man's opinion (and usually their own), they're far from average. (Note: Men do the same thing, though probably not as much as women.) I know that average is in the eyes of the beholder–and given that the average dress size is 14, a lot of women justify their average. Trust me, it's not going to work. Men who have been burned too many times look at "average," see that you've only in-

cluded a head shot, or two, and come to what may be the right conclusion, at least based on their prior experience: She's lying.

Next.

Obviously, there's a simple solution to the problem. Post a current full-body photo of yourself.

If you think you should post a full-body photo only if you have a decent body, think again. In fact, my feeling is: the less conventionally pleasing your body, the more important it is that you post a full-body photo. And by full-body, I really mean from head to toes. Of course, it should be the most flatteringly realistic; it should show how proud you are of how you look. (If you're not proud of how you look, do something about it—before you join an online dating site.)

One of the most pleasing photographs I saw online was an overweight woman in a flattering jogging outfit running along a jogging path. It said (to me), "Here I am. This is really me. So, maybe my weight isn't in proportion to my height, but I take good care of myself, and I'm happy with my body."

So what happens when you check off slender, because you really are? Do you still need to show it in a full-body photo? Answer: Absolutely. Men who have been burned too many times see that you've described yourself as slender, but note that you've only included a head shot, or two. They think, "If she's really slender, why isn't she showing it?" Seeing is believing.

Next.

The bottom line is, no matter what, you need to show what you really look like through your best photos: A close-up headshot and full-body shots in a variety of situations that are reflective of who you truly are.

If you exercise, post a photo of you exercising. If you play the piano, post a photo of you at your piano. If you are truly looking for an animal lover, post a photo of you with your pet. If you love your children and/or grandchildren to death and want to find a

man who isn't turned off by that, post a photo of you with members of your family. Post a photo of yourself in formalwear (but only if you like to dress up); post a photo of you in casual attire, preferably jeans (but only if you look good in jeans), preferably with high heels (but only if you actually are the type who wears jeans with high heels). Let me tell you, men love women in jeans with high heels!

Think of it as a photo shoot. Change the backgrounds Change your clothes.

THE DON'TS

Don't post blurry photos.

Don't post photos that are too dark.

Don't post photos that don't have you in them.

Don't post photos of you without a smile on your face.

Don't post photos of you in the distance.

Don't post photos where you've cut out someone else, even if it's a girlfriend.

Don't post a photo of you with a drink in your hand, unless you really are a heavy drinker.

Don't post a photo of you in a hat. (Men will think you're experiencing hair loss, or worse.)

Don't post a photo of you in sunglasses. (Men will think you're cross-eyed, or worse.)

Don't post just one photo.

Don't post photos from different times of your life.

Don't post photos that are more than two years old, even if you think you haven't aged. (You have.)

Don't post a photo of you without glasses if you wear glasses.

And above all else,

Don't post your profile without photos. Statistics show you will receive twice the number of responses if you post photos than if you don't.

I said in my introduction that you must read this book critically, analytically. That you must decide for yourself what resonates for you and what doesn't. And I still believe that, except in the case of the photographs you post. Of course, I can't force you to do as I say (and as I did), so I'll make the following deal with you:

Post photographs of yourself that are more than two years old and/or photos that don't show your body (especially if you're not slender or average by men's definition of average) and see what happens. How many men take you out for a second time? If you're not happy with your answer, take down the old photos and post a current head shot and a current full-body photo.

Not convinced yet? Maybe this will convince you: I've heard of men getting so irate about women who don't look like their photos that they'll end the date before it begins. As in, "I'm sorry, but you don't look anything like your photo, and I'm really not interested in wasting your time or mine." Others aren't that polite; they simply walk away—turn around and head in the opposite direction—when they realize that the "old bitch" (that's what they'll call you) who's standing outside the restaurant is the person they're supposed to be meeting . . .

Next.

*N*ow, continue to the next chapter, or flip this book over to page 11 to see how I did it.

CHAPTER THREE

Next, The Profile:
How To Do It

Why should you spend a lot of time on your profile, if all that really matters to a man is the photos? I guess I'm going to have to say, "Just because _____" You fill in the blank. You take pride in who you are? You have integrity? You have a strong work ethic, and, after all, finding the man of your dreams is about to become your second career? Aren't you looking for the man out there who will pay attention to what you've written–that you've spelled all the words correctly, written complete sentences, and offered up cogent thoughts? That's the man who will read your profile and say, "Ah, here's someone who really cares. Here's someone good enough to meet."

It's not just about what you write; it's how you write it. No misspellings, no incomplete or run-on sentences. Put commas where they belong. Start the sentence with a capital letter and the rest lower case with a period at the end. Avoid exclamation marks!!! Don't be negative unless you really are a negative person and want to meet someone who's negative, too. There's nothing wrong with writing,

"I'm a worrier, so I'm looking for someone who likes to be worried over."

Trust me, they're out there. No, it's not necessary to give a laundry list of your worries. Save that for the first meeting.

If you say,

"I'm adventurous,"

you better be telling the truth. If you're not adventurous, you're better off saying,

"I love staying home and watching Netflix,"

or if you really do see the glass half empty,

"You'll never catch me skydiving. I'm convinced the parachute won't open."

If you're simply not a good writer, ask for help from someone – a friend – who really knows you.

If you need some inspiration, check out your competition's profiles. You'll gain insights on what to say, and what not to say. Be analytical. Take notes. Write down words, sentences. Look at what you think works, and what you think doesn't work. Try to imagine how a man would perceive and/or interpret what these women wrote. You'll also find it useful to look at men's profiles, not only for what they say about themselves but also for what they say about the women they're looking for. All of this is fascinating research, and time well-spent.

THE DON'TS

The following are turn-offs to men.

Don't make the focus of or lead-in to your profile your commitment to your children, grandchildren, or friends. Why? It'll make

the reader feel as if there's no room for him in your life. Here are some examples from actual profiles:

"What I value most dearly and would be incomplete without is my family and friends."

"My children are an extreme priority."

"Being with my grandchildren is my joy."

"My favorite thing is spending time with my niece."

Now, that doesn't mean that you can't say anything about your family and friends, if they truly are an important part of your life (and will continue to be even after you've met the man of your dreams), but it needs to be tempered. It certainly shouldn't be your opening line.

Don't mention the death of your spouse in your text. You indicate that you're a widow in the marital status section, so there's absolutely no reason to mention it again. Hey, if you were a man, would you be turned on to:

"I have been widowed for two years, and it's time to move on and put myself out there."

Or,

"I have been a widow for nearly five years and have moved on with my life. Life is for the living as my deceased husband told me shortly before he passed away."

Don't be vague. As in,

"I guess you could say that I enjoy all kinds of different things."

Or,

"I am a spontaneous person who is searching for someone to be spontaneous with."

Don't be negative. Some examples:

"Well, I never would have expected, when I was a young woman, that I would be trying to sell myself online to perfect strangers." (Note: This is not only negative, but it makes this person sound really old.)

"My perfect match is not looking for just sex."

"I have no use for a liar."

"I am not a liar."

"I won't expect you to join me, but please refrain from scoffing at my youthful passion." (Huh?)

"I choose not to be around negative people. OK? So please stop now if your cup isn't half full."

"Oh yes, if you get your panties in a bunch over little things, better not call me because I am far from perfect." (Panties?)

Nor would I recommend that you write the following, even though I could definitely relate to the author (I felt her pain)–and applauded her for her honesty:

"If you're the kind of man who halves the bar tab or mapquests the exact distance halfway between you and me. . . you are not the guy for me."

EXCEPTION: There are ways that negatives can work very well. For example, you can write:

"I'm quiet, but not shy; intelligent, but not arrogant."

Don't quote your friends, relatives, or exes (even if you think it's a literary vehicle to describe yourself). No man cares what someone else thinks about you; he wants to know what you think of yourself.

"My friends (mother, sister, ex-husbands) say that I'm attractive, joyous, enthusiastic, vivacious, sensitive, compassionate, loving, sincere, honest, generous, gentle, self-sufficient, sensuous, and understanding."

EXCEPTION: The following, written by a man, is definitely an exception to the rule:

"Some people say that I am loyal, smart, tolerant, funny, fair, attractive, and nice, but they don't know the whole story."

Or, if you're really uncomfortable coming right out with your positive attributes, you can get away with:

"I'd like to believe that I'm an interesting, upbeat person who'd like to meet an attractive, intelligent, witty, and independent counterpart."

Don't live in the past:

"I got married very young and stayed married too long."

Don't state the obvious:

"Please don't contact me if you're still attached or worse yet, married. We'll have nothing in common!"

Don't state the unnecessary:

"If you don't have a photo, don't write because I won't write back."

Or the absurd:

"My mother would say to me as a child that I looked beautiful, but she wanted me to be beautiful on the inside too. I've heard people say that everyone likes me, so I think I've made my mother proud."

Don't say it when you can show it. For example, don't write:

"I have a great sense of humor."

Instead how about something like:

"Everything interests me, with the exception of anchovies on pizza."

Now, senses of humor are, well, funny things. Everyone thinks they have one. It's just that one person's sense of humor isn't someone else's. Maybe the reader won't think the above example is funny. But that's the point. You've put it out there; you've shown it. It's up to the reader to smile, laugh, or . . .

Next.

There is, however, an exception to the show it don't just say it rule, and that is, trying to show how sarcastic you are. If you really want to let the reader know that you're a sarcastic person, it's better to simply say that your sense of humor is on the sarcastic side. Maybe give a couple of examples. The problem with showing sarcasm is that it often gets misinterpreted as bitterness. As in this example:

"You're kidding! You look so much younger. I never would have guessed. Why don't you go to the Red Sox game with the guys? I'll stay home and wash and wax your BMW. I left your toilet seat up for you. Sure, you can have your poker game here. Smoke cigars inside? Super! Fat? You? Not at all. It must be one of those imported shirts. Their sizes are smaller than our sizes."

And please remember, if you really are funny, you don't need to write LOL or :−)

Don't say that you're looking for someone with a sense of humor. Instead, say that you're looking for someone who will make you laugh, and visa versa.

Don't pose questions you really don't want answered.

"What are the odds of meeting that right person (not perfect mind you), but the 'right' one on the internet?"

Don't put your dirty laundry out there.

"This site is UNDER RECONSTRUCTION. Recently I experienced a ride on this Match.com internet dating roller coaster that would make any sane person hit delete and run. I am a sane person . . . but part of my heritage is Scottish and the subscription is paid for awhile . . . hate to waste it!!! I am more convinced than ever that the only way to really decide if you want to know someone is through conversations in person. Just because I mistook ONE of you guys for an honest, sincere, classy man of integrity, should not make me feel the entire world of men are slugs. So, for now, forget the cute one-liners, the flowers sent via email, the travel plans explored online, the

charming text messaging, etc. . . . . and, when you have something important to say, look her in the eyes!"

THE DO'S

The following works:
Do sound positive and upbeat.

"I am relatively new to online dating, but I think it makes sense because it gives you an opportunity to meet people you would ordinarily never meet."

Do motivate the reader to take action.

"Bike riding in the country, hiking in the mountains, dinner with friends. Care to join me?"

or,

"Meeting face-to-face is the best way to decide if you like someone."

Do include information that may be difficult to write about, if you think (know) you should.

"I am a breast cancer survivor. It's not so sexy to bring it up, but it does matter to some people, so I'm putting it out there for those of you who don't feel comfortable with it."

Edit, edit, edit your profile before posting it. Eliminate repetition and "too much information." In the end, the reader should not have to scroll through your profile to get to the end. Here are some examples of information that could/should have been left out:

"I have auburn hair and can burn at the beach."

and,

"My only turn-offs are bad manners, pushiness, and people who drive within the speed limit."

and,

"The last thing I read was the expiration date on my milk carton. It's one of my fears: taking a big gulp of spoiled milk. Ew!"

and especially,

"I love Egyptian cotton."

Analyze, analyze, analyze your profile before posting it. Analyze it from a man's point of view.

Here are some examples of "red flags":

You write: *"I would love to have someone to share my secrets and wishes, someone to rub my neck and shoulders after a stressful day."*
And he thinks: "Way too needy."

You write: *"I am the modern day 'Dear Abby.' Whatever it is, I want to be able to discuss it with you."*
And he thinks: "No thank you. I don't need your advice."

You write: *"I'm lucky that I photograph well."*
And he thinks: "How ugly is she?"

You write: *"We all have some baggage in our lives."*
And he thinks: "Some?"

You write: *"I see life through the eyes of a child."*
And he thinks: "Am I going to have to cut her meat for her?"

You write: *"Don't worry. I won't make you go shopping with me or hold my purse in public."*
And he thinks: "Only old people who have been married too long do things like that."

You write: *"I'm looking for someone to think about when we're apart."*
And he thinks: "Get a life."

BEST ADVICE: Try to write the text of your profile the way you sound. The best way to make it happen is by saying the words out loud. You may feel foolish, but you'll probably be surprised at how easy it makes the process. You can also elicit the help of a friend, and you can recite your profile to him/her while (s)he writes it down, then reads it back to you out loud.

And in terms of content, when in doubt, describing what you're looking for in a man (and in your life) rather than describing who (you think) you are is a lot better. As one man – and he turned out to be my "Mr Right" – wrote after reading my profile,

"Your profile is one of the best I've read because it tells me what you're looking for instead of who you are. Who you are is for others (hopefully me?) to judge."

Re-evaluate your profile every once in a while, if for no other reason than to update it. You don't want men to think you've been on the site forever. Or that you don't care enough to change information that needs updating, like mentioning a favorite restaurant that closed two years ago.

You might also want to make minor changes on an ongoing basis for the following reason: On most online dating sites, making a change bumps you to or toward the top of the profiles shown. That gives you a big advantage over the person whose profile appears on page 20, or worse. A lot of men don't get beyond the first handful of pages when they do a search.

TO LIE OR NOT TO LIE

It's a fact: People lie in their profiles. Women typically lie about their age and their body type/weight. (Men typically lie about their height—and their body type/weight. And their age.)

Now, if your mother was/is anything like mine, you were asked, "And if Jenny jumped off the Brooklyn Bridge, does that mean you should, too?" In this case, the answer can be, "Yes," but only if it's a vehicle to put yourself within the searcher's radar screen. Those lies are easily correctible (and I'll tell you how to do it in the next chapter).

LYING ABOUT YOUR AGE.

When it comes to age, any two-digit number that carries a zero at the end of it is dangerous. Simply put, you simply will be out of the radar screen. Men search for women up to 49, so if you're in your early 50s, stay below the age 50 mark. Men search for women up to 59, so if you're in your early 60s, stay below the age 60 mark.

Rule-of-thumb: It's fine to lie about your age as long as your photos are recent (within two years). Current (under a year) is even better.

LYING ABOUT YOUR MARITAL STATUS.

When it comes to marital status, it's dangerous to say that you're separated, even if you are. The reason: Most men think that a legally separated woman is a) still carrying the torch for her husband (and that could be true); b) too new out of her marriage and shouldn't be dating yet (and that could be true); c) in the throes of a contentious divorce and he could become implicated in the divorce proceedings, or worse (and that could be true).

Women (and men, too) who have never been married often

choose "divorced" because men (and women, too) tend to think there has to be something "wrong" with someone (especially someone "our age") who couldn't hook a spouse.

LYING ABOUT YOUR DRINKING HABITS.

If you don't drink at all because you simply don't like to drink, it's perfectly OK to choose "social drinker." That's because most men think that women who say that they don't drink at all had – and/or still have – a drinking problem.

LYING ABOUT WHERE YOU LIVE.

If you live in an out-of-the-way area, there's nothing wrong with listing the closest metropolitan area because that will give you a broader base of men. But you should only do it if you are willing to do most of the driving.

When you look through other people's profiles, you'll notice that some 'fess up to their lies in the body of their profile.

For example,

"I indicated I was 59, but I'm really 64. I was concerned that I wouldn't fall into your search criteria My photos are recent, though, so hopefully you will agree that age is just a number."

Or,

"I wrote that I drink socially, but I really don't drink at all. It's not because I have a drinking problem; it's just that once I graduated from college and didn't have to get drunk to have a good time, I realized that I really didn't like the taste of liquor. I guess the good news is, I'm a cheap date."

Or,

"I said that I was divorced, but the truth is, I've never been married. I was in a relationship for 20 years, but neither of us wanted kids, so why get married?

What not to lie about? Lying is not a vehicle to turn yourself into someone you're really not and never hope or expect to be. If you're really not an optimistic person, don't say that you see the glass half full because you think men are attracted to upbeat women. They'll see right through you on first contact. If you're not happy being a pessimist, then you need to do something about it – before you go online. If you don't like classical music, don't say that you do because you think men are attracted to women with an erudite ear. If you really like rap, say so; but you can also say, "That doesn't mean I require that you have to like it, too." If you smoke, don't lie about it. Don't even say that you're trying to quit.

Besides coming up with a profile, you also need to come up with a name. It's often easier to wait until you've written your profile. Then, you can decide what the theme is – or the most important point you're trying to make – and turn that into your name. Think of it as writing the title to a book. But don't give yourself a negative name, like *LonelyinBoston* or *NoFunLately*. Men don't want to meet lonely women or women who aren't having any fun. That's way too depressing.

You might want to consider highlighting what's important to you as your name. For example, *4SocialChange* or *LetsTango* or, if you really are a status seeker, *RolexGirl*. Of course, you should think twice about names like *SexKitten* or *Hot4U*, unless it's the message you want to convey. If you can't come up with anything unique, there's always your given name.

If you don't choose a name, the site will do it for you. Don't let that happen.

You could end up with *SIWELFOOFS*, though in this case, you don't have to worry. It's already been assigned to someone else.

Finally, you'll need to come up with a "tag line"—the sub-heading that goes under your name. If you have difficulty with it, go back to reading what your competition has written. It's not about plagiarizing. It's about being inspired and/or extrapolating a theme or concept.

*N*ow, continue to the next chapter, or flip this book over to page 27 to see how *I* did it.

CHAPTER FOUR

Trolling For Men:
How To Do It

STEP ONE: THE SEARCH

It all starts with checking out profiles. Imagine this: All you have to do is choose an age range and mileage parameters, and a whopping 500 men will pop up for your consideration. Five hundred men. Now, that's incredible.

It's an even more heady feeling that, just as you're trolling for men, they're trolling for you.

Always keeping in mind that this is a numbers game, your goal is to explore as broad a base as possible. Think expansively, and cast a wide net. The broader your base, the better your choices—and your chances. Still, you need to make your own decisions about your parameters.

Ask yourself, if I hate to drive, should I keep my geographic parameters within a 15-mile radius? Or should I invest in a driving instructor to give me a refresher course so I'll feel better about driving longer distances?

Ask yourself, "If I'm certain that I would marry only someone who shares my religious background, should I include my religion as a key word when I do my search?" Or, "Should I search for men from a variety of religious backgrounds who could become a good friend, or a fling, or both?

Remember, your parameters can change from one search to another. But in the beginning, you're going to need to set aside several hours to work your way through the maze of photos and profiles. The more you do it, the better you'll become at speeding up the process.

Next.

Soon, you'll be getting through 500 profiles in half the time. In part, your increased speed will be due to the fact that a lot of the same profiles will be popping up every time you do a search. "Been there, seen him."

Next.

In part, it's because you'll become savvier about how the system works. For example, people on Match.com who don't want their profiles seen have to manually "hide" them if their memberships haven't expired. If their memberships have expired, they have to specifically request that their profiles be removed. So when you see that a man hasn't logged on for "over three weeks," you know not to waste your time writing to him. You can assume that he's involved with someone, or he's no longer a member. Even on the off chance that he might return to the site someday, it's still not worth the time or effort. There are too many other fish, actively swimming, in the pond.

Next.

You'll find that you become efficient at honing in on what you need and/or want to find out right upfront that will determine the eligibility criteria you establish for yourself. But even when you become really proficient, your searches should never be during a coffee break or 10 minutes before your favorite television show. That's not taking this job seriously enough.

The beauty of online dating, of course, is that you can eliminate men without ever having to meet them, or even email them. All you have to do is pay attention to what they say in their profiles. Your "deal breakers" will be looking right at you.

Now, it's up to you to decide what your deal breakers are. If you like making lists, by all means, make a list of your deal breakers. Just remember, it's not written in stone. Rather, it's a work in progress. Add to it; delete from it. What time-savers deal breakers can be!

The more men you meet, the more deal breakers you'll probably add to your list. Except when you're at your most desperate, and then you'll probably find yourself making exceptions. Don't be surprised if you regret it. That's not all bad. It can be a good reality check, as in, "I'm getting too desperate" or "I need to take a break" or "It's time to change my parameters" or "I need to rethink my goals."

Ultimately, your list may prove meaningless, but that's OK. Along the way, it will provide you with a crucial framework, an important crutch that you'll rely on to make the journey easier.

Just slightly below deal breakers in importance are turn-offs. Some seem universal. Like the absence of photos. Who wouldn't be turned off by a profile without a photo? Now, you could simply ignore those profiles without photos. Or, a better choice: If you find something compelling about the profile, you could–should–shoot off a quick email requesting some photos. Make sure to ask for current, or at least recent, ones. As in,

Hi: I really enjoyed your profile. Do you have any current–or if not current, then recent (within the last two years)–photos you could send me?

What's important is what photos "say" (to you) about the man. What turns you on? What turns you off? If you're a pet lover,

seeing a photo of a man with his dog should spark your interest. If you're dead-set on a man with a full head of hair, you'll probably want to stay clear of men who show themselves wearing a baseball cap. (But what if it has your favorite team's logo on it?). Of course, to give the guy the benefit of the doubt, you can always send an email asking,

What's under the cap?

Check in with your instincts, your intuition. When you look at a photo, do you have a feeling that the person behind it is nice? Funny? Intelligent? It's amazing what you can sense about a face and/or body. You can certainly tell if the guy cares about the impression he makes. Do you like what he's wearing? Do you think he's standing in front of that boat because he's showing off? Or because he's hoping to find someone who'll share in his special interest?

Pay attention to the names men choose for themselves. It's a great way to get a sense of how clever they are, whether they have a sense of humor, whether they've taken the time to do better than "Bob17." Pay attention to the taglines, too. But pay the closest attention to the text. Be critical. What resonates? What doesn't? Go with your gut.

It isn't just what he says in his profile, but how he says it. Is there a style to his writing? Don't you think that a man who takes the time to write a profile stylishly cares about the impression he's making?

When you read a profile that seems too intense, do you equate that with neediness? Or a lack of sense of humor? Do some profiles give you a sense that the person who wrote it is egocentric? Controlling? Or is he open and honest? (And not because he wrote, "I'm open and honest.")

Be analytical; read between the lines; laugh out loud; make comments out loud (even obscene comments, if you're so inclined).

Play a new game as you're trolling for men. It's called, "What Does He Really mean?" Here's how to play, using real examples:

Under the heading, My Education, you read:

Business major, Syracuse University.

And you say:

He really means *I never graduated, but hopefully you'll never know, and I can pretend I'm something I'm not.*

Under the heading, My Religion, you read:

I'm as certain as can be that each and every 'religion' devised by man had 'gotten it wrong!' but is willing to die to defend their superstitions!

And you say:

He really means *I'm a close-minded, rigid thinker.*

You read:

I was the Chairman of two hotel related firms that I sold over a decade ago (now I just manage my own capital).

And you say:

He really means *Now I'm just full of myself.*

You read:

I'm looking for someone that will share her life and always be there for me, as I will always be there for her.

And you say:

He really means *I'm going to suffocate you.*

You read:

If you have questions about me, I will answer them truthfully to the best of my ability.

And you say:

He really means *I'll come up with lots of excuses when you catch me lying.*

You read:

Here are some stories you can ask me about on our first date.

And you say:
He really means *I'm going to do all the talking.*

He writes:

I'm looking for someone who's willing to work hard at a relationship.

And you say:
He really means *I'm difficult to please.*

You read:

As for the development of relationships: full disclosure requires that I admit to some existing commitments. That said, there are creative possibilities. I believe that in the beginning there is the word, and corresponding is half the fun of exploration.

And you say:
He really means *I'm married.*

See, through it all, you can enjoy the process by making it fun. No matter what, it's your opportunity to "meet" hundreds of men in a matter of hours from the comfort of your home. Think of it as totally entertaining, something to do in your spare time when there's nothing to watch on TV. When you're feeling lonely, read some profiles. It can definitely be recreational, but also–and always–serious and purposeful. You want to meet as many men, who fit within your parameters, as quickly as you can. I've said it before: This is a job. Do it with a positive attitude and a sense of determination.

Never end a search without finding at least five men to contact.

If you can't find at least five, then you're being too picky. Figure out a way to broaden your parameters, or change your goals.

Develop a system when you do your searches. Write down the names of the men you think are worth pursuing, and once you've gone through all of them, go back to the interesting ones and re-read their profiles. If you're still interested, send them an email. On a typically fruitful search, you could be emailing as many as 50 men.

One of them could be your Mr. Right (whatever your definition of Mr. Right is at the time). All have the potential to enhance your life, even briefly, even slightly.

How great is that?

STEP TWO: THE INITIAL CONTACT

You absolutely can't sit back and wait for men to contact you. If you do, you'll be sitting home alone. Most men, especially those of a "certain" age, simply don't need to contact women. They can just sit back and wait for women to contact them. As a rule, then, you'll probably find that the men who do make the initial contact are not men you're going to be interested in. Plus, if you like being in control, you'll certainly feel more in control when you're the one who initiates. So, start sending those emails immediately.

Keep them short, but sweet. Long emails are neither time efficient nor necessary. Worse, they often give the wrong impression, like, "Does this woman have too much time on her hands?" or "I bet this is a form letter that she sends to everyone."

The idea is to send more short emails than fewer long ones. The secret to an enticing initial email is:

Don't say anything about yourself. (You don't need to; it's already in your profile.) Rather, focus on the man you're writing to—in a simple and straightforward format, and a flattering way. Men love to be flattered!

You're welcome to use the heading I always used:

Wow!

The text:

I just read your profile, and it was great (OR: I was so intrigued by it; I was blown away by it; I loved it) — not only what you said but how you said it. I hope you enjoy my profile as much as I enjoyed yours. My name is . . .

That's absolutely all you need, unless there's something that really stood out in his profile, especially something that you and he have in common. Then, by all means, allude to it. In a sentence or two.

Next, wait for a response.

STEP 3: HOPEFULLY, THE RESPONSE

As a rule, you'll probably get responses from about half of the men you write to. Positive responses, that is. If you don't, go back to the drawing board. Figure out what you're doing wrong.

Sometimes, men will send a "thanks, but no thanks" email. Often, it's a canned response that the site provides.

Really, that's totally unnecessary, insulting, a colossal waste of time for both the sender, and for you, and often more disappointing than receiving no response, especially if you've been very turned on to that person's profile.

An email from _____! You get excited. "He wrote back! He wrote back!" And then you open it. He's not interested. How depressing is that!

It isn't like you need an "I'm not interested" email to figure out that someone isn't interested. The absence of a response is a very clear message.

Don't be surprised if you receive a "yes, I'm interested" email, but there's something about it that turns you off. Sometimes the turn-offs are obvious. Too long and boring; obviously formulaic re-

sponses sent to every woman who writes to them; inappropriate re-marks, often with sexual overtones; sarcasm; negativity. Sometimes the turn-offs are subtle; you just have a gut reaction to them—and you need to trust your gut.

The more responses you receive, the more you'll trash. But the idea is to receive as many as you can.

Reminder: It's a numbers game. The right one(s) will come along.

So will the wrong ones—the ones who are looking for an email "pen pal," and, for whatever reason, will never come around to actually meeting you. No thank you! Follow your instincts. Avoid them. Anything more than four emails, and you can figure that he's a loser. Sure, there can be extenuating circumstances. For example, someone is out of town and won't be able to see you for a couple of weeks. But in the meantime, he suggests that you correspond. Your response:

Call me when you return so that we can get together.

If you feel good about the email you've received, the next step is to send an email suggesting, if he hasn't already, that he give you his phone number so you can have a conversation that will, hopefully, lead to setting up a time and place to meet. Or, if you prefer, send him your (cell) phone number, so he can call you.

Like those men who want to be "pen pals," you'll find men who want to become your "phone buddies." Again, no thank you. You have better things to do with your time. Like search for other men who have joined for the same reason you joined. If a man can't commit to a time and place to meet in two phone conversations or less, forget about him. And if you don't like the way he sounds on the phone, be honest.

"I've enjoyed this phone conversation, but I think I'll pass on our getting together."

Another way of saying it:

"I'm afraid I need to get off the phone now."

If he asks about getting together, you can say,

"I'm not sure. Let me give it some thought."

He should get the message.

Phone conversations can be dicey for another reason. On the one hand, you want to get a feel for the guy. On the other hand, you don't want to get too in-depth because then you run the risk of having to answer questions that are best answered when face-to-face, especially if you've lied about your age on your profile.

Be prepared: Men who have been around the dating block a few too many times, *i.e.*, burned too many times by women, will probably ask you pointed questions about your profile during your first phone conversation.

Are your photos recent?
Is that your real age?
Have you told any other lies that I should know about?
Do you have any STDs?

So be prepared. You may end up telling the truth even before "the meeting." Come up with an answer that works. If you're about to confess to your real age, always follow it up with:

But I assure you, my photos really are current (recent), and I certainly don't act my chronological age. I hope you'll agree when we get together.

STEP 4: THE MEETING

In the jargon of online dating, what was once called "the first date" has become, "the meeting." (The next time you get-together, that's "the first date.")

In the beginning, you're bound to be overly optimistic. "This could be the one," you say to yourself. After a while, you become more realistic. But you should never approach it in a negative way;

you should never be thinking, "This is going to be another wasted night." There are no wasted nights. Of course, there are times when you look at the man, and he's twice as wide and half as tall as you expected, but who knows, he may be able to recommend a good plumber (or he may be one), a good hotel in St. Martin, a good book to read, a great buy on a laptop. Or he may become a friend. If nothing else, he's one more frog en route to the prince. One more down, one less to go. Smile. You got out of the house, didn't you? Maybe you even ate at a nice restaurant. Approach it in a negative way, and you'll come across as negative, which becomes a self-fulfilling prophecy. Approach it in a positive way, and you'll come across as positive. That becomes a self-fulfilling prophecy, too.

Of course, unless you have a mind and heart of steel, the meeting will inevitably be a roller coaster ride – from start to finish.

On the one hand, there's the anticipatory excitement:

Wow! I'm going to meet someone new.

On the other hand, there's the anticipatory dread:

Help! I'm going to meet someone new.

On the one hand, there's the giddiness around preparing for the meeting.

What should I wear? I think I'll have my hair done!

On the other hand, there's the trepidation:

What if I trip in these high heels?
What if my deodorant fails me?
Does my hair look OK?
What if he's loud and obnoxious, ugly as sin, a real jerk?
What if he doesn't like me?

Inside, you're absolutely petrified. But you never want to show it. A couple of minutes ahead of time (five minutes if you're really

nervous), take deep steady breaths; think positive (Can you say, "I'll get through this" or "This will be fun" or "I'm psyched"?); smile.

Practice smiling in front of a mirror. Practice laughing. Listen to how you sound when you laugh. Modulate your laugh if you need to. Broaden your smile so that your face lights up and your eyes twinkle.

Talk yourself into it, as you head toward the meeting place: "Smile, smile, smile." It doesn't matter whether you ever see that man again. It's good practice for you.

When a man sees you smiling, he'll smile back. That's a good start. No guarantees, of course, that it will end well, but at least you'll feel as though you've approached it with a positive attitude. First words out of your mouth, "It's so great to meet you." You're looking right into his eyes.

Where to meet? If you have a favorite place (as long as it's not a high-end restaurant and you expect him to pay, or a noisy neighborhood bar where everyone knows your name), it's fine to suggest it, but protocol seems to dictate that the man comes up with a meeting place. Don't be surprised if it's a Starbucks. For coffee. Even if it's not a Starbucks, it's often like a Starbucks, a place for coffee where you order, pay and pick up at the counter. It's not just casual; the guy is pretty much guaranteed that it doesn't have to cost him any money. All he has to do is get there ahead of time and place/pay for his order. You'll find him at a table, waiting for you to join him. But first, you'll have to place/pay for your own order.

Trust me, it can become off-putting after a while, if not right away. Not because you should expect him to foot the bill, but because it reflects on the man. Is he jaded (from too many awful first meetings), or is he just cheap?

An alternative – meeting for drinks at the end of the day – makes a lot of sense because if you're really getting along, you can always extend drinks to dinner. This can be awkward, though, because the potential rejection sort of hovers over the meeting.

You like the guy; you're thinking, "What if he doesn't suggest dinner?"

You don't like the guy; you're thinking, "I hope he doesn't suggest dinner."

Meanwhile, the guy could be thinking, "I'd like to suggest dinner, but what if she says, 'No'?"

The suggestion of lunch or, especially, dinner for the meeting is often seen as risky, because it usually means a longer time commitment — great if you like the person; torturous, if you don't.

With a meal comes the question. Who pays? The best rule-of-thumb: Always be ready, willing and able to pay your share — and always offer. Always be able to pay the entire bill, should the moment arrive. Think: he excuses himself to go to the men's room, then slips out the door. It can happen. Hopefully not to you. According to men, women do it to them. Hopefully, you won't. There are better ways to end the meeting without burning your bridges.

It's generally customary — polite — to spend an hour with the guy even when you know right off the bat that this will go nowhere, that there's no chemistry. It's amazing how instantaneously you'll know it, and it's not just about being turned on physically. It's a mental thing, too, and seemingly impossible to define or explain. So don't even try.

You may hear some men refer to the meeting as the interview. That usually depends on how adept a woman is at asking questions. Not that the men mind the role of the interviewee. Even those who complain about it — jokingly. The ones who are more evolved, or at least think they are, will often say, "I want to hear about you," but before you know it, they're saying, usually in the middle of your sentence, "Interesting. That reminds me of something similar that happened to me the other day."

By the end of the meeting, you'll inevitably know a lot more about him than he knows about you. It works to your advantage when you know that you never want to see the guy again.

First, if you don't want to see him again, why would you want him to know anything about you?

Second, you'll find it a lot easier to ask questions (and tune out during the answers) than to answer questions. Or just ask an open-ended question, and let the man talk. You'll be pleasantly surprised at how much mileage you'll get out of something like:

So, tell me all about yourself.

Third, it won't take you long to get tired of hearing yourself talk about yourself during those first encounters, so it often comes as a relief to not have to talk about yourself.

But if you're thinking that this guy has potential, and you're going to want to see him again, make sure that you tell him your story.

Everyone who participates in online dating needs a story; and if you've lied in your profile and/or you have skeletons in your closet (and who doesn't have a few?), the first time you meet is the time to 'fess up.

It's not to your advantage to withhold information. Contrary to popular belief, the idea of "waiting till he knows me better" simply doesn't work to your advantage.

If a man can't accept what you have to tell him right from the beginning, you shouldn't be interested in him. If you wait to tell him, then expect the following response:

What else are you keeping from me? How do you expect me to trust you?

Does your story include (some of) your other online dating experiences? That's entirely up to you, but I think it should. I think men actually like to hear those stories. Just be upbeat about them, even the horror stories. This is not about, "Woe is me; I can't meet anyone." This is about, "Wow, this is fun. I'm having so many experiences that I never would have had were it not for online dating."

By recounting your prior dating experiences intelligently, you can get some important points across about what you're looking for in a man. Just as you can learn some very important information about a man when he tells you about his prior dating experiences.

Do you talk about your sexual expectations? Definitely. But it's not by saying, "The last man I had sex with was so fabulous I doubt that I'll meet anyone as good." This is about: "I'm really looking forward to getting to know you better."

It's more than telling your story and listening to his. It's a lot more subtle.

Does he make eye contact with you?

When you say something that you think is funny, does he laugh?

Do you think he's funny?

Is he already exhibiting qualities that you think are important in a man?

Is he intelligent in a way that makes you comfortable?

Is he appropriate?

So, the meeting is over. The end can be as nerve-wracking as the beginning. "Does he like me? Do I want him to?" If you can't wait to beat it out the door, can you extricate yourself gracefully and graciously? Can you tell the truth? It's fine to say, "It was great meeting you" without saying "Let's do it again sometime." How do you respond to his asking you, "Can we get together again?" when you really don't want to? In the beginning, you'll probably say, "Sure, I'd love to." It's awkward to say, "You know, I really enjoyed meeting you, but I don't think we're a match" because often a man will ask, "Why?" And there's no point in going there. A middle-of-the-road solution to, "Can we get together again?" is, "Let me think about it."

Here's a tip: If you're going somewhere where there's metered parking, park close to the meeting place and put 90 minutes in the meter. If you want to end your time together when the hour is up,

look at your watch and say, "Oh no, my meter's about to run out. I have to go." If you don't want the time together to end, it's, "Oh no, my meter's about to run out. I have to go put more money in." Of course, if the man is ready to end the time together, you've given him the perfect opening to his saying, "No, that's OK. I need to get going."

Oh well, one more down; one less to go.

When a man ends the meeting with an unenthusiastic, "I'll call you," that usually means, "I'm not interested." But if you are, it never hurts to say, "I really hope you do because I really enjoyed this time together." You can even follow it up with an email. If he doesn't respond, then. . . oh well, at least you tried. It's never about, "Oh no, I blew it; I should have never sent that email." The reality is, you did what you did, and you did it for the right reason. If he wasn't going to call you anyway, the email didn't hurt, and who knows, if he needed to be sure you weren't going to reject him, the email helped. He's probably ended up calling you.

And when it comes right down to it, that's what it's all about. Two people at the end of the meeting who both want to advance to the first date.

*N*ow, continue to the next chapter, or flip this book over to page 61 to see how *I* did it.

CHAPTER FIVE

What About Sex?

Just as you'll make rules for all the other facets of your online dating life, you're going to have to make the rules that work best for you – and only you – about how you deal with sex. Sure, you're going to trust your gut about the men you choose to go out with, and who you choose to sleep with, but that still doesn't mean that you have to throw caution to the wind. Not when the stakes (think: STDs, AIDS) are so high.

Yes, I decided not to have rules about sex, about blood tests, about condoms, about when and with whom. That's why I have no sub-heading for this chapter. No "How To Do It." I'm leaving it up to you to decide what it should be.

I won't be insulted if you call it, "Do As I Say, Not As I Do."

Still, no matter what your rules, you can open yourself up to new possibilities – even those you may fear initially. After all, it's scary. How long has it been since you've had sex with a man? And who was it with? Your ex-husband? A lot has changed since then, and so, I'm sure, has your body. Can you imagine standing naked in front of a man?

No, it's not easy, but if you can change how you define what sex is all about—if you give yourself permission to evolve, it can be extraordinarily liberating and better than you've ever had. Or imagined. Here is yet another opportunity for you to take control. For you to be in charge. For you to accept the way men think about sex (keep reading), and enjoy the pleasure of it—without compromising what's best for you. Reinvent yourself and your sexuality. And you'll feel younger, more vibrant, more creative, more in control, more excited, more exciting, and more enlightened. Open yourself up to new possibilities by defining and even re-defining your ideas about sex. Does sex have to define your relationships? Does the pleasure of it have to be associated with an act of love? Or can it be a stand-alone act with no strings attached? It's entirely up to you to decide.

Go ahead; give it a try. You can always change your mind.

So, what about sex and the man? Well, while you're evolving, he's staying the same. I can practically guarantee it. You'll quickly discover that, no matter what his age, he still thinks with his penis. Ask him. He's not ashamed to admit it. If he's interested in you, it's not (only) about how smart, funny, or rich you are. He looks at you and thinks, "Do I want to have sex with this woman?" And if the answer is, "Yes," his next question is, "How soon?" Only a handful of men are into wanting to get to know you better first.

You'll find that they're much less patient about dragging it out. Maybe it's their "life's too short" way of thinking. Or maybe—probably—it's that "candy store" mentality. As in, "If she's not going to have sex with me, I can find someone else who will. All I have to do is go online, check out profiles. . ." How will you deal with that?

You'll find that if they think they can get you into bed by telling you that they love you, or by sounding more serious about you than they actually are, they'll still say what they think you want to hear. Just like when you were in high school! Don't say that you haven't been forewarned!

You'll find that the men you meet disregard warnings about STDs. You might think they're all going to want to see your blood test results, but very few do. You might think that even – perhaps especially – without blood test results, they're going to insist on wearing condoms, but surprisingly few do.

By the way, ask a man why he doesn't believe in blood tests or condoms, and you might get the following response:

"We all have to die of something."

You're bound to meet the men – and there are a lot of them – who will tell you: "I don't go to bed with women who insist that I wear a condom." They mean it, and the truth is, they don't have to make exceptions for you. There are plenty of women who'll accommodate them. But that doesn't mean you have to break your rules.

You're in control.

*N*ow, continue to the next chapter, or flip this book over to page 69 to see how I did it.

page 69

CHAPTER SIX

Oh, The Men You'll Meet

You'll meet the Henrys and Harrys and Larrys and Garrys/ Garys. Jays, Rays, Michaels, Freds, Teds, and Jeds. And that's just skimming the surface. The poor, the rich, the very rich, and, it'll seem, everything in-between. The self-employed, the under-employed, the unemployed.

Professors, accountants, architects, lawyers, high school teachers, elementary school teachers, producers, directors, new car salesmen, used car salesmen, pilots, ministers, former CIA agents (at least that's what they'll tell you), men with no body hair, men with too much body hair, doctors from every religious denomination. Men with bladder control problems, diabetes, sexual dysfunctions, triple bypass surgery, hearing aids, canes, and if you hang in there long enough, walkers.

Tennis pros, basketball coaches, marathon runners, heartthrobs, heartbreakers, losers, more losers. And, oh yes, winners. You'll definitely meet winners. The big question is, Will they think you're a winner, too? You'll meet men who want to see you again, but you have absolutely no interest in them. You'll feel an instantaneous attraction to a man, and he'll sit through the meeting checking his watch.

Oh, when will the man you like like you?

There'll be so many men you may just have to start giving them nicknames. It's a lot easier—and a lot more fun—to call Ted "Stick Man" because he's so thin; to call Jed "Roller Boy" because he loves to skate; and to call Fred "The Man With All the Toys" because he loves his car, his boat, his newest iPod, and the biggest flat screen TV you've ever seen.

Yes, if you do it right, you'll meet them all: The good, the good-looking; the bad, the ugly. And before it's all over, you'll have made the same mistakes that every other intelligent woman who takes intelligent risks has made. And trust me, you'll be a better person for it.

No matter how smart and savvy you are, you'll ignore warning signs (don't forget, it was a minister—a man of God—who stalked me). You'll turn your back on deal breakers (or adhere to them too stringently); you'll embarrass and humiliate yourself. You'll spend too much time with the wrong man; you'll make too many compromises; you'll believe too many lies (and tell some of your own along the way).

Oh, the men you'll meet will have war stories to tell. Unless you're their first online date, and that's not a good idea (odds are they won't settle for the first one they meet), they'll be veterans of the Dating World War.

Oh, the men you meet will tell you stories about women deceiving them about age, body type, photos. But that's just skimming the surface. There's so much more. It could give you a whole different impression of the men you'll meet. And the women they met. Women who give women a bad name. Shame on them.

If you meet a man who insists on coffee only, and only at a place like Starbucks because he's holding tight to his wallet, it

might not be because he's cheap. He may be the man who has this story to tell:

He was enthralled by the profile of a woman who loved classical music; he loved classical music, too. Towards the end of an animated phone conversion, when both expressed an interest in meeting in person, she suggested that upcoming Friday night. For dinner at a very nice Italian restaurant and a concert.

As he'll tell it:

It was a lot for a first meeting, but we really did have such a good phone conversation. She even volunteered to phone in an order for the tickets, if I would volunteer to pick them up. Of course, I agreed.

I went to the box office to pick up the tickets, which, I assumed, she had already paid for with her credit card. I figured that I'd pay for the dinner, and we'd be "even."

When he got to the box office, the most expensive tickets in the house were being held, but they hadn't been paid for. What could he do?

He'll continue:

I paid for the tickets. What else could I do? I figured, she'll either reimburse me for her ticket, or she'll offer to pay for dinner. But neither happened. In fact, she didn't even volunteer to split the dinner tab. From then on, I made it a rule. Coffee only for the first meeting. Dinner and a concert a lot later. And I don't do box offices.

Or you'll meet the man who wouldn't pick you up at your house, even if you asked. Not until he really gets to know you.

Here's his story:

I really liked this woman the first time I met her, and I was really looking forward to getting together with her again. We planned to have lunch, and we

were going to meet at the restaurant, but at the last minute, she called me and told me that her car was in the shop and would I mind picking her up.

When he picked her up, she told him she had just gotten a call from a local shoe store.

He'll continue:

It seemed that she had ordered a pair of shoes, and they had just arrived. She was all excited, and she made a big deal out of how jealous her girlfriends would be when they saw these shoes. She told me, "I absolutely have to pick them up now. Would you mind very much if we stop on our way to the restaurant?" Why not? I'm a nice guy.

When they arrived at the shoe store, she said, "Come on in. Don't wait in the car."

He went in with her; she tried on the shoes.

"What do you think?" she asked him.

They walked over to the cashier, and she started fumbling through her bag. And fumbling some more. Then she dropped the bomb:

"Oh no," she said to me. "I must have left my wallet and my credit cards at home. Would you mind very much paying for them, and I'll pay you back."

What could I say? I may be a nice guy. But I'm not an idiot.

"Well, could you drive me back to my house?" she asked him when he refused to pay for her shoes.

And he declined again. He figured:

She can call one of her girlfriends to pick her up.

If you're shocked because the man you've met doesn't invite you to spend the night at his place, this may be the reason:

I got an email from this woman online. She wrote that she wanted to get together right away, which was not unlike what she had said in her profile.

Something like, "If you like my profile, send a cell phone number, please. It will put us on fast forward if we are a match. Time is of the essence." Her "Last Book Read" was "How To Make Love All The Time." Her "Favorite Hot Spots" were "Anyplace is hot when you're with the one you love."

He sent her his cell phone number, and she called him, suggesting that they meet in front of a Whole Foods Market where they could sit outside and have something to eat.

He'll continue:

I recognized her as soon as I saw her, but wait. What was she doing with that oversized suitcase at her side? And what was that on her other side? It was a very little dog. I said something like, "What's with the suitcase and the dog?"

There was an explanation, of course. She told him that she had just come into town (Oops. She hadn't mentioned that to him on the phone.) And the place she thought she was going to be staying at wasn't available.

Can you guess what happened next?

During the course of the get-together, she asked him if she might stay at his place.

He'll continue:

I explained to her that I only have one bedroom, that I don't sleep with women on the first date, and that I don't think her spending the night is a good idea. But she didn't let up until I agreed to let her stay. But I told her, it could only be for one night, that she would have to share my bed, and that she had to agree to "no hanky-panky."

She assured him that all of that was fine with her.

And I believed her. I shouldn't have. That night I ended up having to fight her off, and even the next day, in the living room, I had to fight her off. She'd come out of the bedroom, parading herself around the living room, stark naked, asking me questions so that I'd have to look at her. A couple of times, she'd plop herself down on the couch. I'd have to get up. I wasn't playing that game.

One night led to two, and it only got worse. Two nights led to three. That was – finally – the tipping point.

The next morning I told her that she had until 11 a.m., and if she wasn't out, I was going to throw all her clothes out onto the street, and her damn dog, as well.

At 10:50 a.m. some guy knocked on the front door. The two men exchanged pleasantries, and she left. The only thing she left behind was a bathrobe with a Hyatt Regency hotel emblem on it. It fit him perfectly.

Wonder what ever happened to him? I'll tell you.

A couple of months after his unwanted houseguest, he received an email from a woman telling him she had read his profile, and she was interested in meeting him. He checked out her profile and liked what he saw, but there were a lot of red flags. She had a teen-age daughter who lived at home. That was definitely a deal breaker. She spent week-ends horseback riding and even entered competitions. He had never even been on a horse. He had always shied away from the outdoorsy type. He was more the homebody type. She also lived outside his geographic parameters. She was taller than he was, and that had always been a deal breaker for him, too. But he figured:

Hey, she wrote. She liked my profile. I wasn't seeing anyone else. I was having trouble meeting anyone I liked. So I wrote back; I gave her my phone number; she called me; we met.

Three months later he asked her to marry him, and she accepted.

There's an even more interesting back story to this.

She had been reluctant to go online to meet men, even though she hadn't come up with any alternatives. The way she saw it, it would take way too much time and effort. She didn't want to search through hundreds of profiles. She didn't want to compose emails. Her friends cajoled her into it. They pushed and pushed

and pushed until she finally said, "Fine. I'll do it. But I'll do it my way."

And what a way it was.

First, she wrote a short, generic email: "Hi: You look interesting. How about contacting me?" Second, she selected an age range and geographic parameter. Hundreds of men's profiles appeared on her screen. She didn't read any of them. Instead, she sent her email message to every other man. That's right; she didn't read any of the profiles. It was a totally random act!

"What was it about my profile that made you contact me?" her future husband asked her when they met for the first time. She told him the truth.

So, you see, anything's possible. The only rules there are are the ones you make.

Oh, the men you'll meet.

They won't look anything like their photos.

They won't make nearly as much money as they claimed to in their profiles.

They won't have as important a job as they described.

They'll have health problems that they didn't tell you about up front.

They'll be too fat or too thin.

They may like movies, but none that you like.

They'll be shorter than you, but rarely much taller than you.

You never would have responded to their profile, had you known.

They'll have bad table manners.

They'll be crude.

They'll be inappropriate.

They'll embarrass you. (Like asking you, "What did he say?" while you're watching a movie – in a theater, not on TV.)

You won't think their so-called jokes are funny. (But then, they won't think yours are funny either.)

They'll have emotional problems that you'll discover right away (that's the good news) or only after you've dated them for six months (that's the bad news).

They'll have skeletons in their closet that they'll withhold.

You'll trust them until you discover how untrustworthy they are.

They'll be cheap, stubborn, controlling, shallow.

Some may even be married.

They'll disappoint.

And even though you'll give up on each of them (hopefully sooner rather than later), you won't give up.

You'll know that what you want to happen happens not because you want it to, but because you make it happen. In this case, you make it happen by kissing frogs.

Remember, everyone has a number. You just don't know what yours is – until you reach it. And you will.

*N*ow, continue to the next chapter, or flip this book over to page 93 to see how *I* did it.

CHAPTER SEVEN

And You'll Live Happily Ever After

This is how you'll live happily ever after:

You'll live up to your expectations, not down to them.

You'll meet your expectations by making them realistic.

You'll rise to every occasion by being upbeat and always seeing the glass half full.

You'll smile; you'll laugh; you'll embrace optimism.

You'll enlarge your friendship base by not rejecting men simply because they're not "The One."

You'll learn something new on each date, take away something positive from every experience you have, from every man you meet.

You'll network. Need a personal trainer? An accountant? A mortgage broker? A car salesman? Now, you can find ones who just happen to be single, too.

If you can't find any interesting men online to do what you want to do (travel, horseback ride, hike, see a movie), you'll check out interesting women online who share those interests.

You'll set time frames that allow you to accomplish your goals. A good time frame: "I will write to at least five men each week." A bad time frame: "I'll only join for a month and see what happens."

You'll think out of the box.

You'll think expansively and throw out a wide net.

You'll stay calm.

You'll stay focused.

You'll learn something new from everyone you meet.

You'll always be in control.

You'll make your inner voice work for you.

You'll never lose your sense of humor.

You'll see this as a second job, a career, and work hard at it.

You'll trust your instincts.

You'll take intelligent risks.

You'll tell your friends everything, but never worry about what they think.

You'll grow with it.

You'll grow to like yourself better.

You'll become a better person, a more intelligent person, a more insightful person.

You'll feel younger.

You'll keep an open mind.

You'll try new things.

You'll find ways to distinguish yourself from others.

You'll do what's right for you.

You'll be yourself; you'll be someone else. You'll reinvent yourself, more than once. You'll try on new personas, and see how they fit. You'll mix and match them.

You'll take advantage of opportunities.

You'll take the initiative.

You'll do everything with integrity.

You'll be confident in others.

You'll become more confident in yourself.

You'll be enthusiastic.

You'll never burn your bridges.

You'll be polite and ethical.

You'll make rules and revise them.

You'll set goals and change them.

You'll stick with it until you've reached your goals—whatever those goals are.

You'll get better at it.

You'll learn from your mistakes.

You'll repeat some of your mistakes.

You'll fall in love—more than once.

You'll break some hearts.

You'll do it the way that's right for you.

You'll learn that you don't have to think alike to love alike.

You'll meet the men who are right for you.

And,

You'll meet the man who is right for you.

You'll live happily ever after.

I did it; you will, too.